KARAVAN KITCHEN

KARAVAN
KITCHEN

SORAYA BEHESHTI

LANTERN PUBLISHING & MEDIA ● NEW YORK

2021
Lantern Publishing & Media
128 Second Place
Brooklyn, NY 11231
www.lanternpm.org

Printed in the United States of America

Library of Congress Cataloging-in-Publication Data

Names: Beheshti, Soraya, author.
Title: Karvan kitchen / Soraya Beheshti.
Description: Brooklyn, NY : Lantern Publishing & Media, [2021] | Includes index.
Identifiers: LCCN 2021010258 (print) | LCCN 2021010259 (ebook) | ISBN 9781590566008 (hardcover)
   | ISBN 9781590566015 (epub)
Subjects: LCSH: Cooking, Middle Eastern. | LCGFT: Cookbooks.
Classification: LCC TX725.M628 B44 2021 (print) | LCC TX725.M628 (ebook) | DDC 641.5956—dc23
LC record available at https://lccn.loc.gov/2021010258
LC ebook record available at https://lccn.loc.gov/2021010259

EDITOR & ART DIRECTOR
Soraya Beheshti

WRITERS
Nabila Naseeb
Mohammad Rahemah
Shukri Abdikarim
Abderrazaq Noor
Nawal Nusrallah
Hana Mahallati
Ghanim al Sulaiti
Yara Ashkar
Roya Joya
Nada E.
Soraya Beheshti

SPECIAL THANKS
Gaia Foundation
Visualizing Palestine

Roya Joya, *The Farmacy Yoga & Pilates Studio*
Al Nabulsi Family
Mohamed Rahemah
Alice Hattar & the Hattar Family
Mahmoud Al-jabiri
Bashar Ali
Mohammad al Khatib
Hamdi Zarour
Jasmine Al-Hawi
Sama Fraij
Mahmoud Ahwal
Jonathan Schory
Evergreen Cafe, Doha
Margot Peacock, Faramarz and Persia Beheshti
Martin Rowe and the team at Lantern Publishing & Media

CONTACT
soraya@karavanfoundation.org
www.karavanfoundation.org

All images were taken by the author or the Karavan Team, or were obtained under a Creative Commons License or purchased. For information on permissions, contact soraya@karavanfoundation.org. Poetry and personal statements were either obtained from the authors themselves. Further permissions can be found on page 330.

SORAYA BEHESHTI
CEO/FOUNDER, Karavan

Soraya Beheshti is a graduate in Middle Eastern Studies and Anthropology from Columbia University. She is the founder of Karavan, a non-profit organization that leverages innovative blockchain technology to improve the lives of refugees around the world. Karavan was a recipient of the Columbia Innovation Grant and was a semi-finalist for the Tech.Co Startup of the Year competition and the 2018 Hult Prize, the world's largest social venture competition.

Soraya has spent the last few years volunteering at, and researching and working with, refugee camps and refugee communities around Europe and the Middle East. She has studied migration and displacement as part of both of her degrees, and wrote her Anthropology thesis on the impact of economic exclusivity on displaced people, and why blockchain systems such as that which Karavan is creating could pave a new future for refugees and the global community as a whole.

يا بلادي

To my country

I want to feel the warmth

of life under your sun;

to feel the breath

of winds

bringing stories of my ancestors

to my eager ear.

I want to pull the memories

out of my head

and stick them on the pages of a

leather-bound book

like a scrapbook of a life

well lived.

I want to burn them,

only to have the pleasure of making them once more.

Then after,

I would collect the burned ashes

and sprinkle them in my garden

so that when I eat,

I am *nourished* by you;

And that when I breathe,

I receive *courage* from you.

I want to take those pages

and frame them on my wall

to show that

despite it all

I am *proud* of that land.

I am *a part* of that land.

And when the dust settles to some new form,

I will skip stones across the water and ride their ripples

to *return* to that land.

There is nothing like the smell of grandmother's kitchen,

centuries transpired to create a land so rich, and,

no sound like the laughter of playing children

who know nothing of the broken stitches in the world before us woven.

I want to melt the memories into gold

and wear them on a chord around my neck,

so that they will always be near my heart.

I'll stash it under my pillow

so I may visit in my dreams

the home that is no longer mine.

It is not enough

but

it's a start

that precludes an end.

Until the day when free is land

and there is no pain in the right of movement,

I'll savor the food of my mother's hand

and the sweet milk of time to soothe it.

Contents

Beverages

Qishr and Ethiopian Coffee

Grains

Rice, rice, rice!

Sweets

Rosewater, dates, and saffron sweets

INTRODUCTION

"We have come to this strange cultural moment where food is both tool and weapon. I am grateful for it. My entire life I knew, and many others knew, that our daily bread was itself a kind of scripture of our origins, a taste track of our lives. It is a lie that food is just fuel. It has always had layers of meaning, and humans for the most part despise meaningless food."
—**Michael W. Twitty**, *The Cooking Gene*

When I was a child, food was more than a source of sustenance; it was an anchor to cultures I inherited but was separated from. It meant remembrance. It meant connection. It meant meals with my family. It meant Dad was home from work. It meant knowing that my story is larger than just *here* and *now*. Food was a vehicle for an expansion of self and an exercise in scaling—geographical, temporal, social.

When I was six or seven, my mother started giving me cooking lessons. At first, I was just assisting in minor tasks, but gradually, something bigger began to take shape. I started to take pride in my ability to perfectly separate egg yolks from whites, or to withstand the pain of dicing raw onions—something that, to my young eyes, made me a culinary warrior.

Looking back, I realize why these little victories stayed with me so many years. The food we ate was a kind of lived and living almanac of . . . *me*. Of the people, the worlds, and the histories that *made* me. In those days, egg whites meant *Pavlova*, the national dessert of my mother's homeland, New Zealand. The two were synonymous. If I was separating eggs, I knew there were strawberries and kiwis in the fridge—and that, very soon, there would be at least five to ten people at the table to join us (because one never ate Pavlova without company). Similarly, the accumulated hours I spent at the sink, removing the skins of broad beans, could be dissected into plates of *baghali polow*, my mother's favorite Persian dish to cook for us. The lessons I learned from these experiences were more than just "how to cook."

I learned patience, because I knew that the taste of the fresh beans, aromatic dill, and fluffy basmati rice was worth the time and effort it took to make them. I also learned about my Persian heritage. These ingredients became so strongly tethered to it that when I encountered them in other cuisines, I wondered how they knew. *Were they Iranian? Was this "fusion cuisine"?*

It wasn't, but to me, dill—like rosewater, sesame, pomegranates, and saffron—were *Iran*. They were my little secret portals, transporting me to my father's homeland, even to my father. When I ate them, I stepped more confidently into my own identity.

This became ever more important once we moved to New Zealand. The Arab world that I grew up in shared many of the flavors and traditions of Persia. How could it not? The two developed at a time when the world was undivided and uninhibited by the kind of structures we take as "natural" today. I was seven years old, and being Iranian was not easy. I wanted to be just like everyone else at school—but it wasn't long until I realized that being a product of history is something to be proud of. The best and worst parts about me were all fabrics woven into the tapestry of who I was, and the facets of my heritage were the stitches that held it together. In my little village in New Zealand, rediscovering the other side of where I came from gave me new life, and new eyes to see it with. After that breakthrough, I yearned for nothing more than to color it marvelous, each experience a thread in a blanket I would eventually pass to my own children.

Food was one of my most profound teachers. It was on the table, before the desk, where I learned *our story.* Recipes are secrets passed from parent to child over generations. Mothers, like mine, teaching daughters, like me. Every family had their own way of making something, and none was ever as good as grandma's. But beyond that, every dish, being at the crossroads of the silk road trading routes, had writ into it the history of the whole world. The subtle note of a single spice in a dish from a certain province told you what had been traded, and with whom. You could deduce the climate of a place by observing which ingredients were used in its regional dishes, and how each was prepared.

> But beyond that, every dish, being at the crossroads of the silk road trading routes, had writ into it the history of the whole world.

My father was an alchemist in the kitchen. Wherever we were in the world, he would flavor local palates with the most unexpected treasures of both his ancestral and historical repositories. During the Iran–Iraq War, many Iranians fled to seek refuge or to escape military service. They established important diaspora communities all over the world. When my father cooked, one could taste the infusion of all the places he once called home.

In alchemy, the process of transformation renders the input components stronger, better able to withstand the corrosive sands of time. Throughout history, migration has greatly contributed to the culinary arts by infusing local cuisines with innovative elements. My father's dishes did not do disservice to the cultural traditions they borrowed from. They were tributes to them. They transformed his experiences from something metaphysical into something he could share with others.

My father's food was both science and art. Perhaps this was where I developed my tendency to identify not *within* structures or identities, but in the boundaries *between* them. I saw the world not as divided into nations and states and borders, nor as a colorless entity, but as a canvas of spilled ink. More Monet than Mondrian. The running drops didn't ruin the others. They beautified them. When they were in harmony, the colors looked bolder. Brighter. Richer. The sum far greater than its parts.

As humans, we rely on structural categorization to organize the enormity of information we come into contact with. Mnemonic hooks anchor our memories into blocks of time. This is no more true than with new flavors or ingredients, which divide time into before and after we experienced *X*. Time is bent and stretched, dissected and connected, by and with food, shared meals, and shared experiences. Smells take us back to our childhoods, while the traditions they represent take us back much further.

Cooking is the closest thing we have to a universal ritual experience. It is sacred, enchanting, and transformative. Heritage cooking is history, chemistry, meditation, worship, and health in one sacramental act. All over the world, men and women bring the fruits of their labors to the table, where they bring into existence a source of nourishment and pleasure. Using all the elements—fire, water, earth, and air—they transform disparate components into a composite whole. Food plays a sacred role in every spiritual tradition because it is an act of creation, and it is central to all of life.

This is the power of ancestral cuisine.

With its ability to invoke so many senses, tasting the food of another's ancestors can give us a taste of who they are. Tasting the food of our own . . . *well, that takes us home.*

What Is the Karavan Kitchen?

I am many things. A daughter, a sister, a student, twenty-four years old, the founder and CEO of Karavan, and a devoted vegan.

I am *not* a chef.

But this book is not made for chefs. These recipes, as grounding and soulful as they are, were not made *by* chefs. They are artifacts, passed down from generations, each one contributing its own flair. Many of them come from the homes of refugees who've had to leave their homelands in search of safety and security. I had the pleasure of getting to know many families and individuals over the last few years, from whom I learned a multitude of things—these dishes being just a fraction of them.

Some of these recipes were taught to me during the times I spent in refugee camps, both in the Middle East and Europe. Others are my own adaptations of the cuisines I grew up with in the Arab and Muslim world(s). They are endowed with the values I have come to hold dear to my heart: namely, compassion, nourishment, creativity, and wellbeing.

We live in what can be characterized as a cosmopolitan Middle East. Pre-revolution, Iran had become a refuge for many

citizens of its neighbors who were experiencing war or conflict; diplomats from the United States and Europe abounded and established multilingual schools; literature and poetry from India, Afghanistan, and Turkey were read with widespread fervor; European, Asian, and local non-Persian ethnic communities all contributed to a burgeoning urban population and a flourishing cultural scene. I would have a taste of this several decades later, growing up in the Arab

world. I attended a British school, but most people I knew spoke different languages at home. The food we ate was an amalgam of Syrian and South Asian cuisines. I attended Sufi concerts with my father, and celebrated both Eid and Christmas. Generations have contributed their mark to the cultures of our countries. This is how the Middle East has always been, and it's how it will continue, because hospitality and openness are written into who we are.

NO PIECEMEAL SOLUTION IS GOING TO PREVENT THE COLLAPSE OF WHOLE SOCIETIES AND ECOSYSTEMS. . . . A RADICAL RETHINKING OF OUR VALUES, PRIORITIES, AND POLITICAL SYSTEMS IS URGENT.

—MAUDE BARLOW

On Eating and Drinking

Kahlil Gibran, *The Prophet*

Would that you could live on the fragrance of the earth, and like an air plant be sustained by the light.

But since you must kill to eat, and rob the newly born of its mother's milk to quench your thirst, let it then be an act of worship.

And let your board stand an altar on which the pure and the innocent of forest and plain are sacrificed for that which is purer and still more innocent in man.

When you kill a beast, say to him in your heart,

"By the same power that slays you, I too am slain; and I too shall be consumed.

For the law that delivered you into my hand shall deliver me into a mightier hand.

Your blood and my blood is naught but the sap that feeds the tree of heaven."

And when you crush an apple with your teeth, say to it in your heart,

"Your seeds shall live in my body,

And the buds of your tomorrow shall blossom in my heart,

And your fragrance shall be my breath,

And together we shall rejoice through all the seasons."

And in the autumn, when you gather the grapes of your vineyards for the winepress, say in your heart,

"I too am a vineyard, and my fruit shall be gathered for the winepress,

And like new wine I shall be kept in eternal vessels."

And in winter, when you draw the wine, let there be in your heart a song for each cup;

And let there be in the song a remembrance for the autumn days, and for the vineyard, and for the winepress.

Ethical Veganism

This book is not about comparing categories of beings, or dehumanizing any persons. Rather, it is about urging us, all of us, to look beyond our circles and to expand the compassion in our hearts to encompass all who require it. It is about asking each individual to think seriously about their place in the world, and the many ways in which we contribute to, and may resist, structures of institutionalized oppression. It is not about disregarding difference, but rather, appealing for difference not to be the basis for oppression, enslavement, or abuse.

It is a book about choosing kindness whenever and wherever it is possible to do so.

17

Why Vegan?

In the previous section, I explain that adaptation is part of the evolution of all things, including food. What we know as "tradition" is not comprised of static artifacts, unchanged over centuries. "Traditions" are concepts or forms, which have been innovated, modified, and expanded on throughout the years. The cultures they represent are like the desert sands, whose dunes are remolded by the often gentle, sometimes forceful, winds of time. It is the regular flux and flow of life that, if anything, defines the human experience: cross-cultural migration, seasonality, innovation, and the changing nature of trends and ethics.

I have chosen to make this cookbook vegan because, to me, veganism represents an ideological standpoint that resists the same structures responsible for human conflict and displacement. It is more than a diet. It is a lifestyle choice based on a recognition of both responsibility *and* complicity, and a movement away from self-interested ego, exploitation, and prejudice. In eschewing animal products, one resists a pattern of decision-making based on the advancement of one's *own* group (in this case, humans) or the fulfillment of one's *own* impulses at the expense of others. Instead, one brings into being a new ethic of decision-making, established on the ideals of compassion and equity.

I have followed a plant-based diet for nearly eight years, and have witnessed my own transformation many times over. I am healthier, happier, and more in tune with my body and the world around me than I have ever been. But most importantly, I went from being an accessory of the status quo to a renegade actively pursuing the expansion of my circle of compassion to those who did not previously inhabit it. In making these small lifestyle changes, I discovered a voice inside me that I had not heard before. It was not the Soraya I knew or had ever known. It was the voice of consciousness that exists equally within and through all of us; and which endeavors to achieve the peace and dignity of all beings. This voice spoke, and continues to speak, for those who could not speak for themselves, or who were simply not being heard.

I started a vegan recipe blog a few years ago that has since grown to include all matter of content related to sustainable, conscious, and ethical living. I seek not to preach, but rather to present an alternative way of living and being in the world.

Contrary to popular belief, most of the world's cuisines have been largely plant-based. Before the advent of industrial farming, most humans could not afford to eat the small herd of animals they might have had in their possession—if they had any at all. Consuming the flesh of animals was often a sacred experience in which spiritual ordinance by monks, imams, rabbis, or priests was solicited to infuse the ceremony with a ritual power that expressed immense recognition and gratitude for the creature's sacrifice. It was usually reserved for significant occasions, such as weddings.

This can be difficult to undersand for those of us born into a time of "superabundance," where we can obtain almost anything, anytime. One need only go to a supermarket to select one of hundreds, if not thousands, cuts of meat, alienated from the bodies from which they came; preserved and wrapped in a manmade material that will itself commit violence to Earth's delicate environment. The experience is utterly desensitizing, and through it, we train ourselves to become blind to the suffering of those whom we deem undeserving of the rights otherwise reserved for those privileged few we consider "human."

The Human–Animal Rights Connection

"Human beings have capitalized on the silence of animals, just as certain human beings have historically imposed silence on certain other human beings by denying slaves the right to literacy, denying women the right to own property, and denying both the right to vote."—**Gary Steiner**

The term *human rights* seems simple enough. The so-called family of nations delegated representation to a collective body that agreed on a set of principles establishing the basis for a kind of common law, the object of which is the protection of certain liberties. Our humanity, it supposes, is the common element sufficient to unite the entire human species. The permanent encoding of "rights" that are to be upheld with no exceptions, and in all circumstances, evokes a certain sense of timelessness and universality. Noble as it is, a mere glance at the state of the Anthropocene dissipates these claims faster than a cloud of mustard gas, or the quasi-permanent smog that lines many of the world's cities.

It follows, then, that the inequitable distribution of *human* rights, or the rights belonging to *persons*, results from an inequitable attribution of *personhood*. In fact, what emerges is a complex rubric by which individuals are categorized (or not) as deserving of certain protections and "rights" according to a dynamic interplay of global distributions of power (hegemony) and mechanisms of scaling that expand and contract the circle of "brotherhood" to include and exclude those positioned outside of the inner circle.

This mechanism is adopted to exclude individuals on a collective basis on the grounds of differently weighted features of identity: religion, race, class, gender, and species. I have spent several years studying food systems and social systems from within the discipline of anthropology. It is from this position that I assert that finding and accessing ethical sources of production becomes more difficult with each passing day. The nature of the capitalist system leaves most corporations prioritizing profit over ethics, whether by choice or necessity. Moreover, it categorizes living beings as commodities. Whereas animal products were once a by-product of the animal's life, today the loss of lives inherent in animal agriculture is seen as a by-product of the lifecycle of the final product. This is demonstrated aptly in the word *livestock*—literally, *living stock*.

This frame of reference is the same one that permits human injustices to occur as "by-products" of resource extraction and other modes of financial gain. Ideas about social hierarchy are ideologies, or beliefs. They are subjective, and wherever they have contributed to social structures, be they racist, colonial, sexist, or speciecist, we have proven ourselves wrong—though not before many millions of innocent lives were lost.

Values, on the other hand, are sounder bases from which to determine our moral compasses. Values, such as nonviolence, compassion, and mercy, are applied without bias. So long as our ethical codes of behavior are determined by ideologies rather than values, we are bound to prove ourselves wrong time and time again. And it is the most vulnerable in all societies, human and otherwise, who are most burdened with the savagery of our mistakes.

"Being vegan is easy. Are there social pressures that encourage you to continue to eat, wear, and use animal products? Of course there are. But in a patriarchal, racist, homophobic, and ableist society, there are social pressures to participate and engage in sexism, racism, homophobia, and ableism. At some point, you have to decide who you are and what matters morally to you. And once you decide that you regard victimizing vulnerable nonhumans [as] not morally acceptable, it is easy to go and stay vegan."

—**Gary L. Francione**

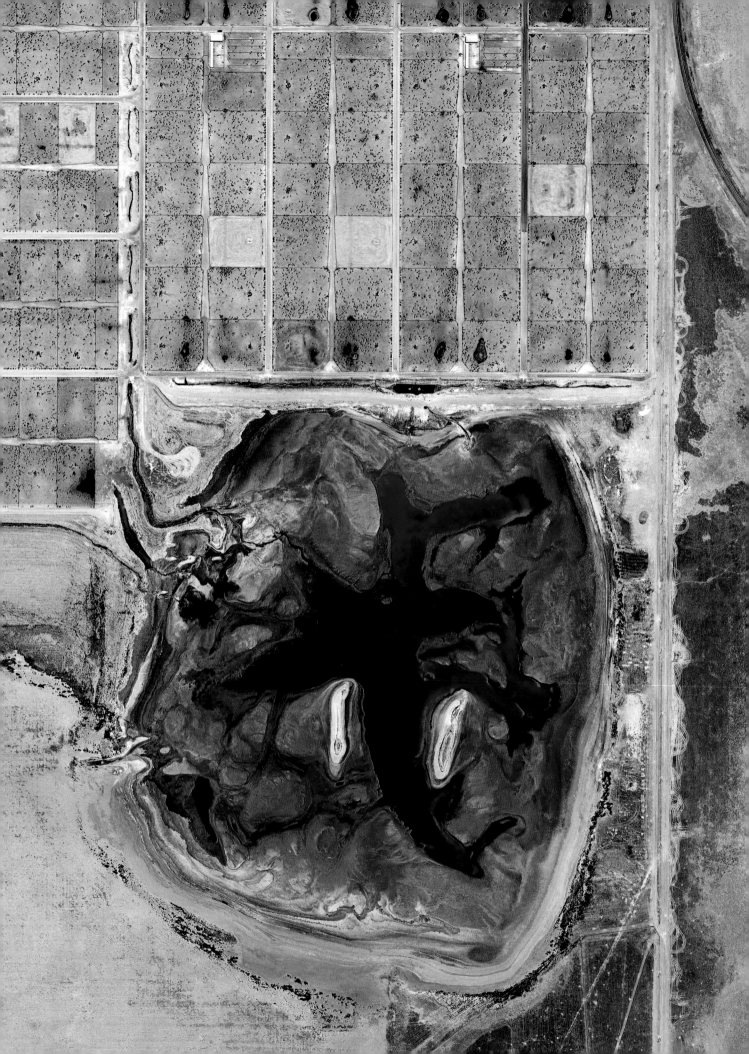

ONLY 100 BILLION PEOPLE HAVE EVER LIVED. SEVEN BILLION PEOPLE LIVE TODAY. AND YET WE TORTURE AND KILL 2 BILLION SENTIENT LIVING BEINGS EVERY WEEK! [TEN THOUSAND] ENTIRE SPECIES ARE WIPED OUT EVERY YEAR BECAUSE OF THE ACTIONS OF ONE AND WE ARE NOW FACING THE SIXTH MASS EXTINCTION IN COSMOLOGICAL HISTORY. IF ANY OTHER ORGANISM DID THIS A BIOLOGIST WOULD WOULD CALL THEM A VIRUS. IT IS A CRIME AGAINST HUMANITY OF UNIMAGINABLE PROPORTIONS.

—PHILIP WOLLEN

Left: Coronado Feeders, Dalhart, Texas (2012). Photo: Mishka Henner, mishkahenner.com
Next Page: Randall County Feedyard, Amarillo, Texas (2013). Photo: Mishka Henner, mishkahenner.com

Isn't man an amazing animal?

He kills wildlife—birds, kangaroos, deer, all kinds of cats, coyotes, beavers, groundhogs, mice, foxes, and dingoes—by the million in order to protect his domestic animals and their feed. Then he kills domestic animals by the billion and eats them. This in turn kills man by the million, because eating all those animals leads to degenerative—and fatal—health conditions like heart disease, kidney disease, and cancer. So then man tortures and kills millions more animals to look for cures for these diseases. Elsewhere, millions of other human beings are being killed by hunger and malnutrition because food they could eat is being used to fatten domestic animals. Meanwhile, some people are dying of sad laughter at the absurdity of man, who kills so easily and so violently, and once a year, sends out cards praying for Peace on Earth.

—C. David Coats

Refugees

A refugee is someone who has been forced to flee their country because of persecution, war, or violence. A refugee has a well-founded fear of persecution for reasons of race, religion, nationality, political opinion, or membership in a particular social group. Most likely, they cannot return home or are afraid to do so.

68.5 million

people have been forced to
flee their homes

That's 28,300 people per day.

Or one every two seconds.

Less time than it takes to read
this.

pp. 38–39: Syrian Refugees. Photo: RomaniaMissions, Pixabay

pp. 40–41: Jetski and Shipwreck. Photo: George Desipris, Unsplash

p. 42: Children in Shinkiari Refugee Camp, Pakistan. Photo: Pixabay

pp. 44–45: Refugees, 2018. Photo: Pixpoetry

p. 46: Afghan child and man. Photo: ArmyAmber, Pixabay

Child Refugees

Children disproportionately constitute the world's population of refugees. They comprise less than a third of the global population, but 53 percent of the world's refugee population.

35 million

children have been displaced by war, conflict, and natural disaster.

1/3

children living outside their countries of birth are refugees.

3.5 million

refugee children are not in school.

53 percent

of refugees are school-aged children under the age of eighteen. Many of these children arrive unaccompanied by adults. Since the process of seeking asylum is incredibly expensive, families may sell all of their assets just to give their children a chance to find safety and security.

86 percent

of refugees are hosted by low-income countries. The only high-income country on the list of the top ten host nations is Germany, coming in at #8, with 669,500 refugees and asylum seekers. The thirty-six most fragile countries account for just two percent of global Gross Domestic Product (GDP), but host 71 percent of the world's population of internally displaced people (IDPs).

66 percent

of refugees come from the following five countries: Syria, Afghanistan, South Sudan, Myanmar, and Somalia.

2.6 million

refugees live in camps. Millions more live in urban areas or informal dwellings.

4,000

refugees died trying to cross the Mediterranean in 2015.

671,000

Rohingya children, men, and women have fled to Bangladesh to escape the massive scale of violence, persecution, and rape in Myanmar since August 2017, making this the fastest growing refugee population in the world.

THE FOOD

SALADS

Saltat Shamandar   55
   Beet salad

Fattoush   57
   Fresh salad with crispy pita croutons

Shirazi salad   59
   Invigorating Persian salad with lemon and herbs

Tabbouleh   61
   Lemony parsley-grain mix

Saltat Shamandar / سلتات شمندار

Beet salad

Serves 4

This simple beet salad makes a great side dish and can be whipped up with fairly little effort. If desired, you may use roasted beets instead of boiled ones. This will add more texture and a deeper sweetness, but will take longer to prepare.

INGREDIENTS

4	large beets
1 bunch	coriander, finely chopped
	salt and pepper, to taste

DRESSING

2	cloves of garlic, crushed
4 T*	olive oil
4 T	red wine vinegar or lemon juice

*T=tablespoon

DIRECTIONS

1. Wash the beets and then bring them to boil in a large saucepan. Turn heat down and cook until the beets are tender and soft (about 30 minutes). Remove from heat and leave to cool.

2. Mix the garlic, oil, and vinegar into a dressing.

3. Peel the beets and chop them into small squares. Pour dressing over. Add salt, pepper, and coriander, and mix.

4. Serve cold and garnish with a few more coriander leaves.

Fattoush / فتوش

Fresh salad with crispy pita croutons

Serves 4-6

Fattoush salad is popular across the Arab world. Although there are regional variations, characteristic elements are the tangy pomegranate syrup and sumac, fresh lemon juice, and crunchy fried pita bread croutons.

INGREDIENTS

3	pita rounds
1 head	romaine lettuce, chopped
2 cups	cucumber
1	red onion
1/4	purple cabbage
6	radishes
2 cups	fresh coriander, chopped
1 cup	fresh mint, chopped
3 tsp	sumac
	olive oil

DRESSING

3	limes, juiced = 6T
1/3 cup	olive oil
4 T	pomegranate molasses

DIRECTIONS

1   Chop the cucumber, tomatoes, red onion, and radishes (without stems) and add to a large bowl.

2   Slice cabbage finely. Add to vegetables along with romaine lettuce, mint, and coriander.

3   Toast pita rounds until they are crispy enough to break into pieces.

4   Heat oil in large pan. When sufficiently hot, fry pita pieces until they are golden brown. Stir to prevent burning.

5   Mix dressing ingredients and pour over salad. Toss until evenly spread and garnish with sumac.

Shirazi salad

Invigorating Persian salad with lemon and herbs

Serves 4-6

This salad goes by many names across the world, though in Persian, it is known as Shirazi salad. It is eaten alongside most meals. It is simple, fresh, and a delicious source of nutrients. Feel free to add whatever other fresh vegetables you have on hand.

INGREDIENTS

3	tomatoes, diced
2 large	cucumbers, diced
1 large	sweet, white onion
3	radishes, sliced finely
1 tsp	sumac powder
2 T	pomegranate molasses
2 T	olive oil
1/2	lemon, juiced = 1 T
	salt and pepper, to taste
optional	garnish with herbs

DIRECTIONS

1   Combine the olive oil, molasses, and lemon juice.

2   Mix the tomatoes, cucumbers, onion, and radish in a bowl. Pour dressing over and mix thoroughly.

3   Add sumac, salt, and pepper, to taste. If possible, allow the flavors to set for an hour before serving.

Tabbouleh

Lemony parsley-grain mix

Serves 4-6

The word tabbouleh *is sometimes believed to come from the Arabic* tabil/tawabil, *which is a designation for ground spices. Thus, the extra-fine chop is an essential characteristic of this salad, whose name can be traced back to the ancient Akkadian language of the Mesapotamian era, when* tabilu *meant "ground."*

As one of the Levant's primary culinary exports to the rest of the world, tabbouleh has been adapted into endless variations. In Syria, tabbouleh is served scooped into lettuce cups. Some ingredients, like red onion and spring onion, can be substituted for each other according to taste. The most typical recipe found in the region, however, is comprised mostly of parsley. Ideally, you would use ultra-fine bulgur, which can be consumed uncooked after 30 minutes of soaking. If this is unaccessible to you, cook the medium-sized variety according to the instructions on the package.

INGREDIENTS

250g / 9 oz flat leaf parsley, stems removed

30g / 1 oz mint leaves

50g / 2 oz fine bulgur wheat

1 red onion or 1 bunch spring onions

1 tomato

2 lemons, juiced = 4 T

4 T extra virgin olive oil

salt and pepper, to taste

sumac, to taste

DIRECTIONS

1 Soak the bulgur in cold water for 30 minutes, until soft.

2 Wash and chop the parsley, tomato, onion, and mint very finely, using a sharp knife. Careful knifework will help the components maintain freshness for longer.

3 Drain the bulgur and add it to the parsley along with the lemon juice, olive oil, salt, pepper, and sumac. Mix and then leave for 30 minutes, giving the flavors time to settle.

4 Serve cold and garnish with a few more coriander leaves.

Mezze and Dips

Mezze is an important concept in Middle Eastern cuisine. It refers to the tradition of presenting a selection of small plates, dips, salads, and appetizers that are meant to be shared among two or more individuals. It facilitates community and diversity—groups of people coming together to savor a wide variety of flavors and dishes, which, owing to their diversity, can accommodate a great number of dietary requirements or restrictions. People of different religions, belief systems, and preferences can come together over *mezze*, and each one will find themselves satisfied, contented, and cared for.

Bread is the central component of *mezze*; a blank canvas on which the flavors, textures, and hues of individual dips or dishes can be expressed. Surrounding the warm flatbread are dishes of vibrantly colored hot and cold *mezze* plates, including the dips you will find in the following pages.

63

Dips, Spreads, and Sauces

Coconut Yogurt and *Labneh*

A dairy-free alternative from Yara in Palestine

Thank you to Yara in Palestine for this delicious, plant-based alternative to both yogurt and labneh. Labneh is probably the only dairy product regularly consumed across the Middle East. It is similar to Greek yogurt, and is made by straining regular yogurt, thus resulting in a thick and creamy consistency. This version uses a combination of coconut milk and probiotics to recreate the same texture and health benefits, minus the negative effects of dairy products. You can find probiotics in the vitamin section of any supermarket or health store.

INGREDIENTS—PROBIOTIC COCONUT YOGURT

1 15-oz can full fat coconut milk

1 probiotic capsule (minimum 25 billion CFU or equivalent in weaker-strength capsules)

INGREDIENTS—LABNEH

1 cup probiotic coconut yogurt

100g / 3 1/2 oz tofu

salt, to taste

olive oil, *zaatar* (to garnish)

EQUIPMENT

wooden spoon

glass jar with cap

cheesecloth

DIRECTIONS

For Coconut Yogurt

1   Empty the content of the probiotic capsule in the jar. Add the coconut milk and stir, using a wooden spoon.

2   Cover the jar with the cheesecloth and leave it on the windowsill for 2–3 days. Then, store the labneh in the fridge.

For Labneh

3   Blend all ingredients until smooth.

4   Serve with a drizzle of Palestinian extra virgin olive oil and a generous sprinkling of *zaatar* alongside vegetable crudités, toasted pita bread, and olives for an authentic culinary experience.

My mother used to get dry chickpeas and soak them in water for a whole day before leaving them to slowly boil on a small fire for about three hours, waiting for them to soften. With her hands, she would then do her motherly magic tricks and grind them together with the right amount of hand-made tahini, lemon, cumin, salt, and water. It tasted perfect every time. I remember she always garnished the dish with chickpeas, pomegranate molasses, and Syrian olive oil, which has a very unique taste.

Zayt alzaytun (زيت الزيتون)—the Arabic words for olive oil—was first a native of Syria before spreading to the rest of the Mediterranean. In fact, the first olive tree came from the ancient Syrian kingdom of Elba, so the legend goes. . . . The cultivation of olive trees is one of the oldest signs of civilization—even older than writing! Almost 6,000 years since it was first cultivated, up until the war, Syrians were still among the leading producers of olive oil. And we use it in all our dishes. Because it just makes everything taste so good. Simple.

—**Mohammed**, Syria, founder of @mos_eggs, London

Hummus

The most famous culinary export of the Levant

Serves 4-6

The perfect hummus. The dish that can literally bring people from all over the world together in lemony bliss! While the beauty of hummus is in its simplicity, made from just a handful of plant-based ingredients, taking it from good to great is all in the details. Remove the skin from your chickpeas to make the blend smoother and use a good quality tahini made from roasted (not raw) sesame seeds. You can make this hummus ahead of time and keep it in an airtight container for a few days. It will thicken in the fridge.

INGREDIENTS

2 1/2 cups	cooked or canned chickpeas, drained
1/2 cup	aquafaba (chickpea water/broth)
1/4 cup	extra virgin olive oil
1/2 cup	lemon juice
1/2 tsp	baking powder
1 tsp	salt*
2/3 cup	tahini
3	cloves of garlic, peeled
1	lemon, juiced = 2 T
1 tsp	cumin
1 tsp	paprika

GARNISH

Finely chopped coriander or basil

Toasted pine nuts

Paprika or chili powder

Zaatar

Pomegranate kernels

Raw or caramelized onion

DIRECTIONS

1   Blend all ingredients in a high-powered food processor, adding some chickpea water as needed to produce a smooth paste. You may need to stop and scrape the sides once or twice.

2   Add salt, pepper, and more lemon juice to taste.

3   Spoon into a serving bowl and create a "moat" to hold the olive oil. Drizzle the oil liberally over the top and garnish with your choice of chickpeas, pine nuts, cumin, paprika, herbs, and chili.

* Mediterranean salt is lower in sodium chloride than regular table salt. Therefore, you may need to use more of the former to impart the same salinity as conventional salt. Mediterranean salt is also richer in potassium, iodine, and magnesium.

Muhammara / سلتات شمندار

Red pepper and walnut dip

Serves 4-6

Traditionally, muhammara would be made by hand with a pestle and mortar. This gives it a beautiful texture that melts in your mouth. But if you are pressed for time, it can be done with a food processor, too. Serve at room temperature with warm pita.

INGREDIENTS

4	red bell peppers
1 cup	breadcrumbs
3 T	pomegranate molasses
1 tsp	cumin
1/2	lemon, juiced = 1 T
1 T	dried chili flakes
1	clove of garlic, minced
1/2 cup	walnuts, crushed
2 T	extra virgin olive oil
pinch	salt

DIRECTIONS

1 Preheat the oven to 200C/390F. Roast your peppers for 15 minutes and then flip them. Return to heat for another 20 minutes. The skin should be blackened and the flesh, soft. When they have cooled down, remove the skin and seeds.

2 Crush the peppers with the breadcrumbs, pomegranate molasses, chili, garlic, cumin, and the juice of the lemon. If you're using a food processor, pulse them until they have blended, but maintain a coarse texture.

3 Mix the crushed walnuts, salt, and olive oil into the paste.

4 Serve cold and garnish with a few coriander leaves.

Lemony Tahini Sauce

A Middle Eastern staple

Tahini sauce is a cornerstone of Levantine food. All across Syria, Palestine, Jordan, and Lebanon, one will find a variation of this sauce accompanying most meals. The ingredients are per serve, so multiply the numbers by the amount of servings you need. Serve over salad, falafels, roasted vegetables, or grains.

INGREDIENTS (per serving)

2 T tahini

1 lemon, juiced = 2 T

3 cloves of garlic, crushed

salt, to taste

DIRECTIONS

1 Blend all ingredients until smooth. Keep blending until the sauce appears lighter in color, creamier, and fluffier.

2 Taste the mixture. There is some flexibility required here because variations in quality and consistency are inevitable when using fresh ingredients. Additionally, you should adjust according to your own personal taste. The perfect tahini sauce should not have an overwhelming garlicky taste; it should have a tangy kick from the lemon, and a thick, but runny texture.

Garlic Sauce / *Toum*

A versatile, creamy addition to any dish

....

Garlic sauce, or toum, *is an extremely versatile and common addition to the Levantine* mezze *table. Fresh garlic is preferable to its powdered counterpart. Raw garlic gives the sauce strong flavor, but also acts as an emulsifier when blended smooth. The texture is therefore creamy but with none of the added animal fats or cholesterol of other spreads, such as mayonnaise. Spread* toum *in sandwiches, or add it to vegetables, rice, or pasta.* Toum *is traditionally made with a pestle and mortar, but I've included directions for using a food processor as well. The sauce should last one month if refrigerated in an airtight container or jar.*

....

INGREDIENTS

1 cup	garlic cloves, peeled
2 tsp	Himalayan or organic salt
2	lemons, juiced
1/4 cup	ice water
3 cups	olive oil

DIRECTIONS

1   Cut the garlic cloves in half and remove the germs from the center.

2   If using a food processor, pulse the garlic with the salt, occasionally topping to scrape down the sides with a rubber spatula, until minced.

3   Add one tablespoon of lemon juice and process for 10 seconds. Repeat with another tablespoon of lemon juice and blend until a smooth paste has formed.

4   Keep the food processor running as you *slowly* pour in 1/2 cup of olive oil, followed by one tablespoon of lemon juice. Repeat this step until all the lemon juice has been incorporated, and then continue with the ice water.

5   The *toum* should be smooth and fluffy. If it feels too thick or heavy, keep blending it. The longer you blend, the more aerated (and therefore fluffy) the mixture becomes. When it has reached a desirable consistency, transfer to a covered jar and store in the refrigerator for up to one month.

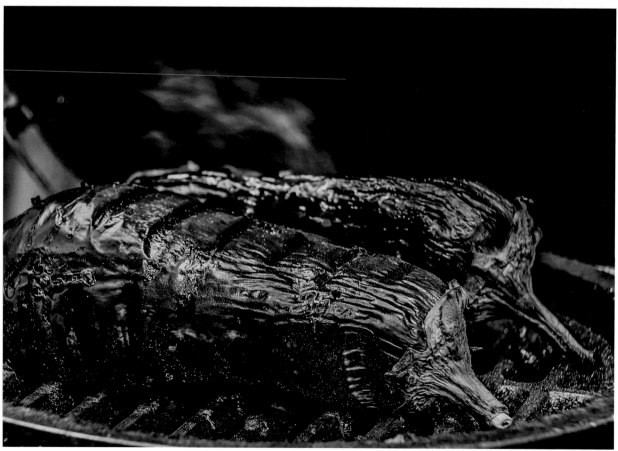

Babaghanoush and *Moutabel*

Eggplants are a widely used ingredient in Middle Eastern dishes. They are savored for their mouthwatering, silky texture and hearty flavor. Scholars believe that eggplant has been growing in what is known as the Fertile Crescent for millennia. According to Assyriologist Jean Bottero, who wrote the book *The Oldest Cuisine in the World*, eggplant was offered at a feast put on by King Ashurnasirpal II as early as the ninth century BCE.

The Islamic world has one of the richest archives of ancient cookbooks in the world, with more Arabic cookbooks dating before 1400 CE than all other languages combined. The oldest in record is called *Kitab al-Tabikh*. It was compiled in the tenth century CE from the recipe collections of the eighth- and ninth-century courts. Other cuisines certainly existed, but the Medieval Arabs took particular care to write recipes down, as well as to transmit them orally. This practice was probably inherited from the Sassanian-Persian court, which was advanced in the gastronomic arts. Thenceforth, the caliphs of Baghdad adopted many of the practices they encountered in Persian kitchens and courts.

Cookbooks from this era celebrate the luscious qualities of the eggplant with abundant dishes in which they are the primary ingredient. The mandrake, of which the eggplant is a relation (and sometimes shares the same name in Arabic, *luffah*), has been associated with alchemy, magic, and medicine for a long time. In the Medieval sources, the vegetable is referred to as both *luffah* and *badenjan*, the word used today. The English word "eggplant" may be derived from this older version, which is thought to have meant "egg of spirits," or *baidh-al-jinn*.

Moutabel and babaghanoush are often used interchangably overseas, but despite being based on the same, luscious ingredient, these are two different dips. Moutabel is creamier, with tahini, garlic, and sometimes yogurt; babaghanoush is fresh and zesty thanks to the lemon and pomegranate molasses.

Babaghanoush

Serves 6

Babaghanoush, *loosely translated, means "pampered father." Its origins are indeterminate, but it can be found across the Levant, the Gulf, Turkey, and North Africa. It is defined by its smoky flavor.*

INGREDIENTS

3	eggplants
4 T	tahini
1 tsp	salt
3	cloves of garlic, minced
2	lemons, juiced = 4 T
1 T	pomegranate molasses
pinch	dried paprika
	black pepper, to taste

ADD-INS

1	tomato, diced
1/2	onion, diced
1/2	red pepper/capsicum pepper, diced finely
2 T	parsley, chopped very finely
2–3 T	walnuts
	pomegranate kernels
1 T	extra virgin olive oil

DIRECTIONS

1 Roast the eggplants whole over an open flame, rotating them periodically so that the outside is entirely charred. The insides should be soft, barely encased by the delicate, blackened skin.

2 Remove them from the heat and leave to cool in a colander/sieve. Then, gently peel the skin off and transfer the innards to a bowl. Use a fork to mash them into a paste.

3 Stir in the other ingredients except for the olive oil and transfer to your serving dish.

4 Use the back of a teaspoon to create a ring around the center of the dip. This will hold the olive oil, which you can drizzle carefully over the top.

5 Serve warm or cold with an extra drizzle of olive oil and enjoy with hot pita bread.

Moutabel

Serves 6

This smoky eggplant dip can be found on mezze *tables across the region, with each culture contributing their own variations. Sometimes it is made with yogurt or tahini; sometimes with neither. Whichever way you prefer to make it, the best product results from eggplants that are charred over an open flame. If you aren't able to do this, you may use an oven.*

INGREDIENTS

3	eggplants
3 T	tahini
3 T	yogurt (use coconut yogurt for a dairy-free alternative)
1 T	extra virgin olive oil
1 tsp	salt
1	clove of garlic, minced
1	lemon
	dried chili flakes, to taste
	black pepper, to taste
	coriander leaves, to taste

ADD-INS

1	tomato, diced
	parsley
	extra virgin olive oil

DIRECTIONS

1   Roast the eggplants whole over an open flame, rotating them periodically so that the outside is entirely charred. The insides will be soft, barely encased by the delicate, blackened skin.

2   Allow the eggplants to drain and cool in a colander/sieve. Then, gently peel the skins off. Transfer the flesh to a bowl and mash with a fork.

3   Add the minced garlic, yogurt, tahini, and salt. You may use a food processor or blender if you desire a smooth consistency. After it reaches your preferred texture, mix in the lemon juice gradually, tasting it as you go to allow for adjustment. Transfer into your serving bowl.

4   Serve cold or hot garnish with a few coriander leaves.

Zhoug

A Yemeni green chili sauce

Zhoug (spelled in a number of different ways) is a very typical Yemeni condiment. The etymology of the name zhoug, *meaning "ground," is similar to that of the Italian* pesto/pestare, *also meaning "crushed" or "ground." It is usually green, although there are red and brown varieties made by adding red chilies and tomatoes, respectively. This sauce is fresh, fiery, garlicky, herby, zesty, and almost totally raw. Use it as a dip for bread, in sandwiches, as a marinade, or to enhance the flavors of other dishes. You can also add mint, which is a variation typically constrained to South Yemen. Like with other recipes in this book, using a pestle and mortar results in the most flavorsome product, but for the sake of convenience, you may use a food processor. Grinding your own fresh, whole spices will also enhance the flavor greatly. Give it a try and see for yourself how much more you can get out of your food when the ingredients are as unprocessed as possible.*

INGREDIENTS (per serving)

1 bunch	coriander, fresh
1 bunch	parsley, fresh = 2 oz
3	cloves of garlic
4	green birds-eye or serrano peppers
1/2 tsp	cumin, ground
1/2 tsp	coriander, ground
1/2 tsp	cardamom, ground
3 T	extra virgin olive oil
3 T	lemon juice, fresh = 1 1/2 lemons
1/2 tsp	black pepper, freshly ground
2 T	water
pinch	salt
optional	small handful of mint leaves

DIRECTIONS

1   Rinse the herbs well in a sieve, especially if they are not organic. Be gentle in your handling of them.

2   Pulse all ingredients in a food processor. The consistency should reach a paste—but you don't want it to be blended smooth. A coarse texture is necessary for an authentic recreation of Yemeni zhoug. If you'd like, you may use a pestle and mortar, instead of a food processor to grind both the whole seeds—making sure to remove any husks—and the rest of the ingredients.

3   Refrigerate in an airtight container. Use it in soups, as a dip, mixed into rice, or spread on a sandwich.

Breads

Falafel Sandwich

The humble falafel sandwich is a staple in many Middle Eastern countries. I grew up eating this at least once a week for most of my life, and the exquisite, unique blend of flavors—tangy from the lemon, creamy from the tahini sauce, and crunchy from the raw vegetables and falafel—never fails to transport me back to those summer evenings in my childhood when we would pick up falafels on the way home after a long day in the sun.

INGREDIENTS (adjust to your liking)

pita bread

falafel (p. 262).

tahini sauce (p. 75)

garlic sauce (p. 77)

tomato, sliced

lettuce, chopped

coriander, chopped

cucumber, chopped

chili sauce, or *shatta*

DIRECTIONS

1 Slice the pita in half so that it forms two semi-circular "pockets." If the bread is not fresh, cover it with a cloth and warm in the microwave for 12 seconds.

2 Fill with hot falafel, raw veggies, and herbs. Drizzle with tahini sauce, *toum* garlic sauce, and any other condiments that you fancy!

Zaatar Manakish

The zaatar manakish *(or* man'ouche*) is another classic childhood favorite across the Middle East—particularly the Levant. I learned this recipe while staying with a Palestinian family on the bank of the River Jordan, though I'd had it plenty of times before growing up in the region. It's super easy, but absolutely scrumptious! Once you try it, you'll never be able to give it up. Plus, it's made with healthy, wholesome ingredients with no cholesterol or animal fat.*

INGREDIENTS

pita bread

olive oil

zaatar

salt, to taste

pepper, to taste

DIRECTIONS

1   Brush one side of a large, fresh pita round with olive oil.

2   Sprinkle the *zaatar* on the oily side of the pita. Use the back of a spoon to smooth it out.

3   Fold the pita round in half so that the *zaatar* side is the interior.

4   Heat a frying pan with some olive oil and fry the *manakish* until golden brown on both sides. Then, transfer the hot pockets to a plate lined with paper towels and serve hot.

Iraqi *Samboosas*

Iraqi-style samosas stuffed with pomegranate-mint mixture (gluten-free option)

Serves 8-10

Although samosas are most commonly attributed to Indian cuisine, they actually originated, somewhat, in the Middle East. The Indian samosa is a descendent of the samboosa, *as it was known prior to the tenth century in Persian and Arabic. One of the earliest mentions of samboosa was in the* Tarikh-e Beyhaghi, *or the* History of [Abolfazl] Beyhaqi *(a Persian historian). Samboosas were introduced to the Indian subcontinent in the thirteenth or fourteenth century by Central Asian traders along the Silk Road. Their presence in India is first mentioned in the fourteenth century by the scholar and royal poet of the Delhi Court, Amir Khusro. Around the same time, Ibn Battuta, the famous Berber-Moroccan traveler, included samboosas in a description of a court meal. Containing almonds, pistachios, walnuts, and spices, these "samosas" more closely resembled Middle Eastern samboosas than contemporary Indian samosas. Other versions of the samboosa have found their way across the world, from Ethiopia and Sudan to areas of Central and South Asia. This recipe, however, evokes the Mesopotamian palette with luscious rosewater, mint, onions, garlic, spices, and pomegranate molasses. Its flavor is unusual, yet mouthwatering. You may substitute the ground beef for a vegetarian equivalent, as I have. Additionally, you can use mini tortillas, wonton wrappers, or empanada wrappers as the pastry in order to save time.*

INGREDIENTS

40ml	olive oil = 8 tsp
2 1/2 cups	cooked ground beef vegan equivalent
1	large white onion, diced
3	cloves of garlic, minced
1 tsp	allspice
1/2 tsp	caraway
1/2 tsp	turmeric
1 tsp	cinnamon
4 T	finely chopped mint
40ml	pomegranate molasses = 8 tsp
2 T	sumac powder
1/2 cup	toasted almond pieces and/or pine nuts
	salt and pepper, to taste
1 pack	wonton or empanada wrappers

DIRECTIONS

1   Heat the oil in a nonstick saucepan or pot on medium-high with turmeric, allspice, caraway, cinnamon, and garlic. Add the onion and sauté until semi-translucent.

2   Add the meat, mint, sumac, and pomegranate molasses. Cook for 5 minutes, stirring with a wooden spoon. Mix in salt, pepper, and nuts.

TO ASSEMBLE

3   Heat a deep fryer or large pot with enough olive oil to immerse the samboosas completely. While the oil is heating, start filling the dough.

4   Place a spoonful of mixture in the middle of a wrapper. Fold the sides into the middle at three separate points, forming a pyramid. Press the edges together as much as possible to seal the pastry.

5   Deep fry in hot oil until crispy and brown. Drain off excess oil and serve hot.

Vegetables

Amharic

አትክልቶች

ātikilitochi

Bengali

শাকসবজি

Śākasabaji

Burmese

ဟင်းသီးဟင်းရွက်များ

hainnseehainnrwat myarr

Kurdish

SEB

Punjabi

ਸਬਜ਼ੀ

Sabazī

Arabic

خضروات

Pashto

سبزیان

Somali

KHUDAARTA

Farsi

سبزیجات

Hausa

KAYAN LAMBU

French

LÉGUMES

Swahili

MBOGA

Vegetable Dishes and Mains

Zaatar Roasted Eggplant with Tahini

Served with creamy coconut yogurt and nutty grains

Serves 4

Zaatar is a very versatile seasoning. It adds depth to the simplest of meals, this one included. The eggplant is roasted until tender, imbued with flavor from the spices and oil. Cross-hatching the eggplant allows the flavors to really sink into its flesh so that each bite delivers a juicy, well-seasoned mouthful. Add cooked quinoa, bulgur, rice, nuts, and dried fruit to turn this veggie dish into a hearty main course.

INGREDIENTS

2	eggplants
4 T	olive oil
1/4 tsp	salt, to taste
1/4 tsp	pepper, to taste
2 T	*zaatar*

GARNISH

1/3 cup	tahini sauce (p. 75)
2 T	pine nuts
handful	coriander or mint
	grain–nut mix (see Directions #5)
optional	dollop of yogurt or coconut yogurt (p. 67)

DIRECTIONS

1   Soak the eggplants in salted water. This will help to eliminate some of the bitterness. After 12 minutes, rinse off the salt water.

2   Mix the *zaatar*, salt, pepper, and olive oil in a cup or small bowl.

3   Make diagonal cross-cuts into the flesh of each half, as you would cut a mango. Brush with the olive oil–*zaatar* mix.

4   Roast for 40 minutes, until the flesh is soft and tender. Check the consistency with your fork. If the eggplant is still a little firm, return it to the oven, checking on it every five minutes until it is delectably soft.

5   Optional: mix cooked grains, nuts, seeds, and chopped dried fruit with 1 tsp olive oil and heat until warm. Serve with the hot eggplant and drizzle with tahini sauce, nuts, herbs, and a dollop of yogurt (see the recipe for homemade coconut yogurt on p. 67).

Ful Medames (Fava beans)

Serves 2-4

The creamy and warm cumin-infused fava beans complement the crunchy fresh vegetables perfectly to create a hearty breakfast dish that comes together in minutes. This recipe was contributed by Nada E., of OneArabVegan.com. Her website is full of incredibly delicious, plant-based recipes, including many traditional, Arabic dishes.

INGREDIENTS

1 can	fava beans = 15 oz
1/2–3/4 cup	water
1	tomato, diced
1/2	red onion, diced
1	clove of garlic, minced
1 small	cucumber, diced
2–3 T	parsley, finely chopped
1/2 T	ground cumin
1 T	extra virgin olive oil
1 T	tahini
1 T	lime juice
	salt & pepper, to taste

DIRECTIONS

1   Start by draining and rinsing your canned beans, before adding to a medium-sized pan on low heat along with the water.

2   Using a fork or potato masher, mash the beans roughly until there are very few whole beans left. Stir in more water as needed along with the garlic, cumin, salt, and pepper. Allow the mixture to heat thoroughly for a few minutes before turning off the heat.

3   Stir in your chopped veggies, parsley, lime juice, and olive oil. Taste and adjust seasonings as needed.

4   Finish with a tablespoon of tahini on top and serve with your bread of choice.

Kousa Mahshi / Stuffed Zucchini

Dishes comprised of vegetables filled with fragrant rice, stewed fruit, and nuts have been served across the Islamic world and Mediterranean for centuries. Aside from zucchini, or *kousa*, stuffed vegetables such as eggplant, tomatoes, onions, cabbage leaves, and vine leaves can be found all over the region during the warm summer months, as well as at communal celebrations like weddings and parties. I learned this recipe while at an *Iftar* (the fast-breaking meal during Ramadan) in Jordan. My hosts had kept the recipe, having inherited it from their elder family members who were forcibly expelled from Palestine many decades before. The night we made these, all three generations of women in the household prepared the food collectively, sharing cups of tea and discussing contemporary affairs. The process is a sacred ritual, an act of community that functions to preserve a history and heritage that global powers insist does not exist.

Every family or household has their own way of making *kousa mahshi*, and it is not something that can be easily attributed to any one place. Although it is sometimes made with ground beef, this recipe has also enjoyed long cultural significance as a vegetarian dish, with plump raisins, fresh mint, and dark, rich greens.

This recipe is nutrient-dense, using many greens and healthy plant proteins. Zucchini contains Vitamins A, B1, B6, and B2; folate; magnesium; potassium; copper; zinc; phosphorus; and protein. Parsley is rich in iron; vitamins K, C, and A; and folic acid. Tomatoes contain vitamins C and E, as well as beta carotene, manganese, and vitamin E. Add the fresh lemon and you have a powerful anti-inflammatory, anti-oxidant recipe.

Kousa Mahshi / Stuffed Zucchini

Serves 6

INGREDIENTS

10	small zucchini
4 T	olive oil
	salt and pepper, to taste

INGREDIENTS—STUFFING

2 T	olive oil
1	onion, minced
4	cloves of garlic, minced
1 cup	short grain rice, rinsed
2 cups	vegetable broth
	salt and pepper, to taste
1/4 cup	pine nuts
1/2 cup	raisins, soaked in a little hot water
1 large	tomato, diced finely
1 bunch	spinach, chopped
1 bunch	fresh parsley, chopped finely
1	lemon, juiced = 2 T

INGREDIENTS—SAUCE

1 can	chopped tomatoes, drained = 14.5 oz
1/2	onion, diced
2	cloves of garlic, minced
2 T	olive oil
1 tsp	ground cumin
2 T	honey or vegan equivalent
1/2 tsp	cinnamon
handful	fresh mint, chopped
3/4 cup	water
	salt and pepper, to taste

DIRECTIONS

STUFFING

1   Heat a frying pan on low-medium heat with olive oil. Add onion and garlic and cook until onions are translucent.

2   Add the washed rice and cook, stirring regularly, for 4–5 minutes.

3   Season with salt and pepper, and add broth. Stir, and then cook, covered, over low heat for 45 minutes.

4   Meanwhile, in a small frying pan, toast the pine nuts and raisins on low-medium heat with 1 T of olive oil. Stir this mix into the cooked rice, along with the tomato, spinach, parsley, and lemon juice.

SAUCE

5   Heat the olive oil in a large pan over medium heat. When hot, add the onion and garlic and cook until semi-translucent.

6   Add the cumin, cinnamon, honey, and mint. Stir and cook for 3–5 minutes.

7   Add the canned tomatoes and reduce heat to low and cook, covered, for 12–15 minutes, stirring occasionally.

TO ASSEMBLE

8   In some countries, zucchini can be purchased with their cores removed. The instrument designed to do this is known in Arabic as a *manakra*. If this is not available to you, simply cut off one end of the small, bulbous squash and use a knife to carefully remove the insides, leaving 1/4-inch of shell. You may save the flesh to add to stews or rice.

9   Stuff the hollowed-out zucchini with the rice mix to three-quarters full.

10   Pour a third of the tomato souce into the bottom of a large saucepan or casserole dish. Arrange the zucchini vertically with the open side facing up. If the zucchini are leaning ever so slightly at an angle, they will cook faster and more evenly.

11   Pour the water and the rest of the tomato sauce over the top. Bring to a boil and then turn down heat, cover, and simmer for 35 minutes longer. The exact timings will change depending on the size of the zucchini, the type of rice, and so forth. As general guidelines, the zucchini should be tender, the rice fully cooked and fluffy.

12   Serve on a platter or plated individually with sauce poured over.

AFGHANISTAN

Afghanistan is a country with a long and rich history. It is the home of the lapis lazuli crystal mines, the Hindu Kush mountain range, several ethnic and linguistic groups, and also the birthplace of the most celebrated and widely read poet in the entire world, Jalaluddin Rumi.

Its vast and diverse landscape allows for a multitude of crops to be grown in the area, contributing a solid foundation for a rich and unique culinary tradition to flourish. The diversity in food also reflects the ethnic and geographic variation across this big and beautiful country. The main homegrown staples are wheat, maize, barley, rice, fresh and dried fruit, yogurt, nuts, and vegetables.

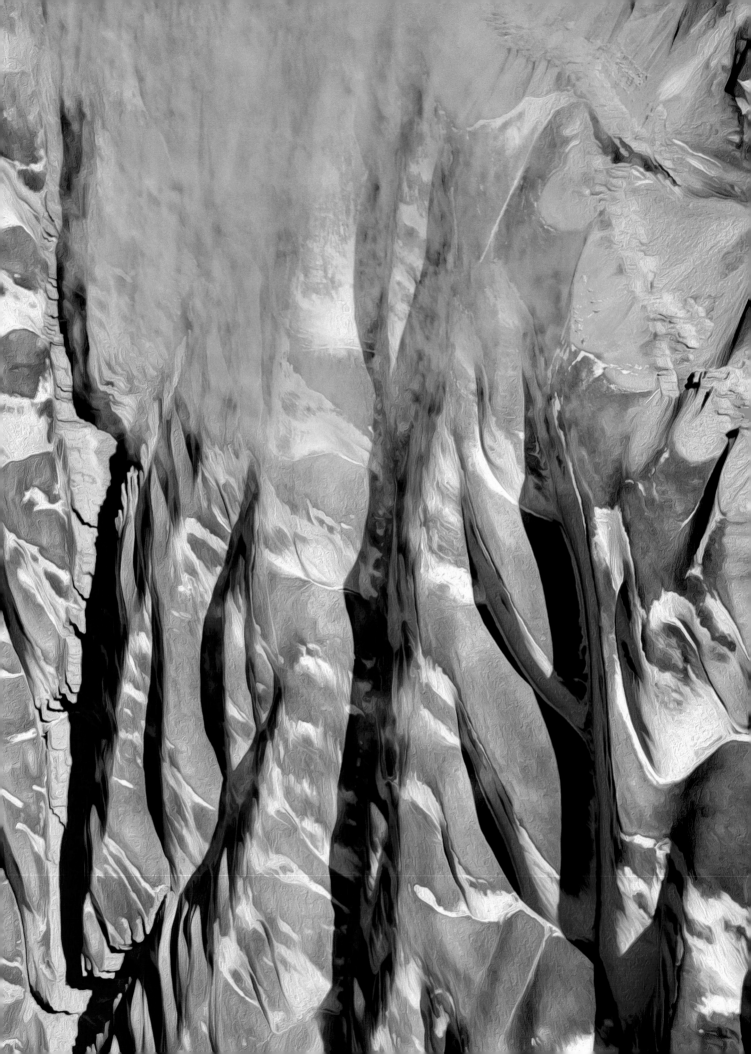

The numbers

- UNHCR reports three million registered Afghan refugees. However, many Afghans live undocumented, making the actual number likely much higher.

- Six million Afghans fled to Iran and Pakistan, where the majority of Afghan refugees still live.

- After Syria, Afghans account for the second-largest refugee group.

- 1.2 million people are internally displaced persons (IDPs) inside Afghanistan.

- Currently, only 15 percent of the population has access to basic healthcare.

After more than thirty years of war, the survival of this rich and beautiful culture is inextricable from the ability of survivors to carry it. Millions of people have been displaced from Afghanistan. The support from the international community has been insufficient relative to the amount of funds, arms, and political support injected *into* the conflict that produced these refugees. Two invasions, countless insurgencies, and generations of disrupted youth have engraved rich scars on one of the world's brightest gems. Europe has adopted a hardline policy against Afghan asylum seekers, and has deported tens of thousands back to a country still suffering under war, occupation, and political instability. Family separations are all-too-common a story in the life of the Afghan asylee. Millions of Afghan refugees live in Iran and Pakistan, though they are increasingly sent away as economic hardships grow more severe in both countries. In other countries, like Australia and Indonesia, documented abuse and negligence are abundant, with refugees living like prisoners in many cases. Here, they may sometimes turn to suicide as a last resort to escape the suffering to which they are subject.

Left: An Afghan girl eats candy while she observes U.S. Soldiers from the 4 Th Battalion, 23rd Infantry Regiment, 5th Brigade, 2nd Infantry Division conduct a joint patrol with Afghan national army soldiers in Shabila Kalan, Zabul province, Afghanistan, Nov. 30, 2009. Photo: Tech. Sgt. Efren Lopez, U.S. Air Force. Creative Commons Public License https://flic.kr/p/7kQ7fh. This photo has been edited.

شعر

Poetry

Poetry, like food, is a unifying force in Afghanistan. It is enjoyed across all of society, young and old. The poetic tradition in Afghanistan extends several thousand years into history, and occupies a revered position today. The cultural repertoires of Afghan literophiles extends far and wide, from the poetry of Rustam and the *Shah Nama* to the wild accounts of Kings Arthur and Henry. When children begin school, the first Persian text introduced to them is *The Divan of Hafez*. Then, they learn Saadi, Bedil, and Ferdowsi. Nor can one exclude the homegrown talent, with the beloved Khushal Khan Khattak bestowed the honorific of the national poet of Afghanistan. In recent years, these cultural delights have become much more difficult to sustain as cultural, economic, social, and political pressures take their toll.

Poetry Battles (شعر جنگ)

Poetry battles, or *sher jangi,* are competitions wherein two participants freestyle to reign victorious as poetry king. One competitor composes a line and the opponent must respond by composing a subsequent line beginning with the last letter of the previous line. This volley continues until either competitor falters too long, and the game is lost.

Illegal Immigrant

it is possible

the sun has risen

and over the mountains

the clouds are there still,

that winds are driving

and families arriving

and there is the sound of a party

sound of dancing, chanting,

and glasses smashing,

the laughter exploding

in every minute and people

and happiness and also

me, with my big heart,

in a ship or strapped under

the truck, I am crossing

the border and moment

by moment am entering

with glory England

—Reza Mohammadi
Aghanistan, Iran

Landai Poetry

Landai is an ancient form of oral poetry dating back thousands of years. It is used to express passionate emotions, such as love and grief between women, particularly Pashtun women. The tradition began with farmers and nomads, who would often sing around a fire after a day of traveling, harvesting, or celebrating. These poems are inconspicuous and anonymous, allowing for audacious, spirited confessions of emotion, and later, expressions of defiance against an increasingly devastating war. This latter development represents the appropriation of an ancient form to express new kinds of grief. In the poem below, the writer compares the feeling of being the one upon whom blame is impressed in a romantic relationship, even when it is the other who has acted hurtfully:

> *My darling you are just like America,*
> *you are guilty, I apologize*

They are community-building, as women use this art to share their most intimate sentiments as individuals, or to grieve the losses of their loved ones and homeland as a collective. Landai poems are composed of two, sometimes-rhyming verses, equalling twenty-two syllables. The word *landai* means "short, poisonous snake" in Pashto—a reference to the common use of sarcasm and wit in the couplets. Despite the clever jabs and brazen quips they sometimes make, the landai poem's rhythm is enchanting. Its steady lullaby pacifies the listener into a sleepy reverie. In that quiet place, deep in the ocean of one's soul, one can not only *listen*, but truly *hear*.

> *When sisters sit together, they always praise their brothers.*
> *When brothers sit together, they sell their sisters to others.*

Women utilize this poetic form, commenting on difficult subjects like war and sex, to challenge the men in their lives or in society, as well as social conventions. The Pashtun women who articulate them are proud, fierce, and unafraid to stand their grounds.

Unlike the high literary Persian and Arabic forms, which can be lofty and inaccessible to many people, landai poetry is *by* and *for* all women. Traditionally, these poems are recited aloud to the beat of hand drums, although this was banned from 1996 to 2001. For centuries, oral traditions were the paramount form of literary output. Beyond literature, the oral form was central to non-formal education, the sharing and development of beliefs and social norms, and the preservation of cultural artifacts. Some trace the exact origin of landai poetry to the Bronze-Age trading caravans moving along the Silk Road from 1700 BCE. The call-and-response mode of communication necessitated by these camel trains may have evolved into the landai form we know today.

Jalaluddin Rumi

Do you know what you are?

You are a manuscript of a divine letter.

You are a mirror reflecting a noble face.

This universe is not outside of you.

Look inside yourself;

everything that you want,

you are already that.

Afghanistan, Iran, and Turkey vie to "claim" Rumi, the world's most beloved poet, as their own. Rumi does not "belong" to any of these states, for they did not exist during his time. He belonged to an age of poets and scholars that roamed the world relatively freely, unconstrained by the borders, passports, and visas that would surely limit them today. Our contemporary conceptions of identity, nationalist and issued by the state, are thus wholly incompatible with those of figures such as Rumi.

The beloved Mowlana Jalal Al-Din Muhammad al-Balkhi thumma al-Rumi (Rumi) was born in Balkh, Afghanistan to Tajik parents. Balkh was incorporated into the Persian Empire, and Rumi wrote most of his work in Dari Persian. It is most similar to the contemporary Dari language spoken in Afghanistan, though it is close to contemporary Farsi. Later in life, he moved to Rum, part of present-day Turkey, where he composed a great number of works. Rumi referred to himself differently at various times, sometimes considering himself "Turk," at other times, "Balkhi."

Rumi was a universal figure whose works of poetry and philosophy explored complex metaphysical concepts, granting their readers unmediated access to a divine realm. In the undeniable beauty of the spiritual world he beheld, the trivialities and injustices of this one are lost. As a Sufi, Rumi was beyond restrictive, nationalist identities. Nevertheless, he is the spoken heart and soul of Afghans, Iranians, and Turks alike. In fact, anyone who quietens their racing mind enough will hear him in the minds of their hearts, no matter where they are in the world.

Afghani *Gulpea*

Stewed cauliflower with ginger, garlic, and tomatoes

Serves 4

Onions, ginger, garlic—delicately spiced and stewed with succulent cauliflower florets—this dish is absolutely heavenly. Serve it on the side of some fluffy Afghan rice (chellow) with pickles and bread.

INGREDIENTS

1 large	white onion, diced
1/3 cup	canola oil
2	cloves of garlic, minced
1 tsp	ground turmeric
1 T	ground coriander
4	tomatoes
1/3 cup	tomato paste
1 head	cauliflower, cut into florets
1/2 cup	vegetable broth
	salt and pepper, to taste

DIRECTIONS

1 Heat the oil in a crockpot over medium heat. When it's sizzling hot, add the onion and fry over medium heat until translucent. Add spices, garlic, salt, and pepper and cook for a few more minutes, allowing the onions to caramelize.

2 Meanwhile, pulse the tomatoes briefly in a food processor. Mix with tomato paste and add to the onion.

3 Stir and cook for ten more minutes on medium-low. You should have a thick, onion-rich gravy. Add the vegetable broth and stir.

4 Place the florets stem-side down into the sauce, pouring some over the top of the cauliflower. Cover and reduce heat. Leave to cook without stirring until cauliflower is tender—usually about 25 minutes, depending on how large the pieces are. It is important to keep the lid on the pot so the steam does not escape.

5 Cook for another 5 minutes uncovered to allow the sauce to reduce. You want the cauliflower to be cooked but not mushy.

Reza

My name is Reza and I am an Afghan refugee.

I am 26 years old, and I am racially a Hazara from Afghanistan. I have been here in Indonesia since October 2014 when I was forced to leave Afghanistan.

I left my school when I was 14 and started working as a car mechanic, but I had to leave my family because of threats from the Taliban.

I made my journey from Pakistan, to Thailand, to Malaysia, and then arrived in Indonesia. I registered in the UNHCR office in Jakarta. And immigration moved me here to Pontianak detention center. I am the oldest son in my family. My work in Afghanistan was as a mechanic. Back at home I have five sisters, all of whom are younger than I am. It has been about 45 months since I saw them last.

Here, there are two kinds of refugees. One kind is those who have economic supporters from outside this country. They can rent a home and buy food and other essentials, and are free to go anywhere around the city. The UNHCR has no responsibility for them, and their refugee process is a lot smoother than the "other" kind. The other kind of refugees have no supporters, and must surrender to the immigration services. Immigration brings them into the camp or detention center. They must accept the life of a prisoner. They are confined to their camp.

I am that "other" kind.

In December 2016, one of the UNHCR members came here and told us we should be "more patient than we think." He said we may be here for ten years, and if we can't tolerate it, we should "go back to our country." In other words, prison or the Taliban. After two years, I have got my refugee status from UNHCR. I am fit and healthy and will do any kind of work. I am learning English in the camp, from teachers who are also here. Fitness is one way I focus my energy. It's my only true escape.

My dream is to be with my family in the safe country.

Nabila

Everywhere around the world, food brings people together. In Afghanistan, a country that is constantly bleeding and in mourning, food provides refuge and comfort. Meals and teatime are when families and friends can sit together, laugh, and celebrate their lives. For me, a refugee and immigrant in the U.S., food was often the only thing connecting me to my home. Coming home from school, my mother always had an Afghan dish prepared that allowed me to retain some of the culture I had left behind.

Later, it felt like I had come home when I ate the same dishes in Kabul. Every morning I would wake to the sound of street vendors selling deifferent foods in the morning. Kabuli palow, mantu, kabob, salads, and some of the best fresh fruit welcome you. Almost everything is organic and bought fresh daily from the street bazaars. Our large family would gather and eat and speak for what felt like hours with food at the center unifying us.

Hospitality is of utmost importance in Afghanistan, so you are bound to be invited for a meal or for tea. Afghans like to say, "If I have bread, tea, and good company, then I have everything in the world." Overall, food fosters community and the simple act of enjoying a meal with loved ones can bring the most light to the darkest spaces.

—Nabila

Kabul, Columbia University, New York City

MASHHAD

Sorkh

Fariman

 A S A N

Torbat-e
ydariyeh   Torbat-e
             Jam

nōbād   Khvāf

Ghurian   Herāt

H   E   R   Āt

Daryācheh-i
Namakzār
Yazdān

Sa   Koshk-e Kohneh

Kūh
3588   Owbeh

Tulak

Shindand

A   F   G   H

Farāh

F   A   R   Ā   H

Daulat   Khāneh

DAYKONDI
GHAZNI
Ghazni
ORUZGAN
Makur
▲3787
PAKTĪKĀ
Mūsa Qal'eh
Qalāt
Mashūray
Arghandab
ZABOL
Khugiani
Kandahār
Ma'ruf
KANDAHAR

Qorma-e-Zardaloo

Dried apricot and herb stew from Afghanistan

Serves 4

Summer in Afghanistan means peaches, apricots, the world's sweetest cherries and fresh, juicy melon. In the winter, when these products are not available, they can be used in dried form to add flavor to stews, or qormas.

INGREDIENTS

2 cups	dried apricots, soaked for 1 hour in hot water
1/4 cup	canola oil
1 large	white onion, diced
1 T	cumin
1-inch piece	ginger, minced
3 stalks	celery, sliced
3	cloves of garlic, minced
2 cups	vegetable broth
1 large bunch	coriander, chopped
1 T	date syrup
2 lemons	juiced = 4 T

DIRECTIONS

1 Heat oil in a saucepan over medium heat. Sauté onion, cumin, ginger, and garlic until caramelized and golden brown.

2 Add broth and celery and simmer covered until the celery is tender—around 15 minutes.

3 Drain apricots (save the water for drinking because it retains a lot of the beautiful, sweet flavor of the apricots) and add to the celery mixture, along with the coriander, date syrup, and the lemon juice. Mix and cover.

4 Reduce heat to low and allow to simmer for 25 minutes.

5 Serve hot with challow, salad, and warm flatbread.

YEMEN

At the time of writing, Yemen is suffering the most severe famine in the world. Prior to the war, Yemen imported 90 percent of its foodstuffs. As a result of the blockades and airstrikes, very little food or aid is now able to enter the country.

In Yemen, like in many Middle Eastern countries, eating with one's hands is a means of connecting more viscerally with one's food. It forces one to be present, eat more slowly, and be more mindful. As you enjoy the delicious food of this ancient culture, please take a moment to think of those in whose hands it should also be, who are today starving. By all means, enjoy the abundance of these recipes—Yemeni people have always meant for them to be enjoyed—but remain ever mindful of those who have been making them for centuries, and are now, for the most part, forced into starvation.

140

Yemen: History

For centuries, Yemen was the Arabian heart of commerce and activity. Sana'a and Aden were great medieval centers for the trade of spices, perfumes, textiles, frankincense, and myrrh, while prominent caravan towns and forts developed in the East. This position has played no small influence on the country's unfolding history. Although much of the population today lives in poverty, Yemen has seen periods of immense prosperity. It was known to ancient Romans as *Arabia Felix* ("Prosperous Arabia"). The mud-brick towers of cities like Shibam, known as the Manhattan of the Desert, are considered "the oldest 'skyscrapers' in the world," sometimes reaching 11 stories.

The area known today as Yemen was host to number of ancient Kingdoms: It was the home of the famed Queen of Sheba. The Kings of Saba (*Sheba* in the Bible) built the Ma'rib Dam in 700 BCE. This dam made possible the development of a robust agricultural supply, which fed the bustling market towns along the coast. The Port of Aden was one of the most important trading hubs in the world, connecting the Mediterranean, India, Africa, and the Persian Gulf. For this reason, Yemen became a melting pot of cultures and religions. It possessed one of the oldest Christian communities, as well as a significant Jewish population. One of Yemen's monarchs converted to Judaism, and Yemeni Jews have historically made major contributions to Yemeni cultural and social life. Islam came to Yemen later, in the seventh century. The Persian governor, along with local sheikhs and their followers, converted to Islam, whether as Shi'ites or as Sunnis. In addition, Yemenis formed diaspora communities in other port cities, including those in Spain, China, India, and other parts of the Middle East and Africa.

Yemen was occupied by both Britain and the Ottoman Empire in the nineteenth century, with the two parties agreeing to divide the country and rule jointly for the remainder of the twentieth century. A small section gained independence following the imperial collapses at the end of World War I—though the British retained control over large parts of the country until 1967. Subsequent power struggles ensued, with foreign powers vying for proxy control of the people and land, including the USSR, Saudi Arabia, Iran, the US, and others. Today, in part because of the apathetic (and sometimes brutal) involvement of foreign powers, Yemen is the poorest country in the Middle East. The recent uprising and war has only aggravated an already dire situation. Nevertheless, Yemen is a country of much beauty: with vast, rocky mountains; fertile green vallies; budding wildflowers; and crystal-clear streams.

pp. 138–139: View of Central Sanaa City Old Town Skyline in Yemen. Photo: TravelPhotography, Adobe Stock

Opposite: Shibam, Yemen. Photos by: Dan. Creative Commons Public License https://flic.kr/p/4u3hxX. These photos have been edited.

p. 142: Al Saleh Mosque in Sanaa, Yemen. Photo: Adobe Stock

The numbers

- 21 million people, or 82 percent of the population, require urgent humanitarian assistance.

- 18 million people are food-insecure.

- Two million children are critically malnourished.

- Nearly 267,000 people have left as refugees to surrounding countries.

- 2.4 million people are internally displaced and unable to leave—nearly 10 percent of the population.

- 14 million Yemenis do not have access to healthcare services.

- More than 700,000 South Koreans filed an online petition urging the government to cease its visa-free policy for Yemenis. Previously, 550 Yemenis had sought asylum on the island of Jeju. Protesters have demanded they be deported.

Yemeni *Saltah*

A succulent stew cooked in a stoneware pot

Serves 4

....

This dish is served with hulba *on top.* Hulba *is a classic Yemeni condiment made of whipped fenugreek and spices. Yemeni* saltah *is distinguished from other stews comprised of similar ingredients by the addition of* hulba *and the use of a stoneware pot. It is comforting, hearty, and absolutely delightful to eat. Garnish with fried onions, herbs, and a drizzle of Yemeni* zhoug *chili sauce (p. 85).*

....

INGREDIENTS

1 tsp	olive oil
3	cloves of garlic, minced
1/2	white onion, diced
1	green chili, chopped
2	tomatoes
1/2 tsp	coriander, ground
1/4 tsp	cumin seeds
1/4 tsp	black pepper, ground
4	pieces of okra, chopped
1	potato, chopped
1 small	squash (e.g. pumpkin), chopped
2 1/4 cups	water
	hulba
	salt and pepper, to taste

DIRECTIONS

1   Heat the oil in a large pan over medium heat. When it is sizzling hot, add the coriander and cumin seeds. Tempering the spices this way releases the essential oils, thus enhancing the flavors of the spices.

2   Add the chopped onion, garlic, and green chili and sauté until the onions have browned—about 8 minutes.

3   Chop the tomatoes and add them to the pan. Cook for about 5 minutes. The water from the tomatoes should have evaporated somewhat. Ideally, the remaining oil has colored a red hue, indicating a rich flavor.

4   Next, add the potatoes, okra, squash, and 1 1/4 cups water. Cover and allow to bubble away on medium heat for 20–30 more minutes. Take care not to allow the vegetables to burn by stirring the pot occasionally with a wooden spoon. The potatoes should be tender and the stew should be thick.

5   The next step is what distinguishes *saltah* from other vegetable stews with similar ingredients. Transport the stewed vegetables to a stoneware pot (make sure it's safe to use on top of a stove—certain varieties may crack).

6   Use the back of a fork to break the vegetables into even smaller pieces. Add a cup of water, salt, and pepper. Mix until combined.

7   Serve bubbling hot with *hulba* (fenugreek paste) poured over, caramelized onion, chopped raw onion, herbs, and a few slices of chopped green chili or a drizzle of *zhoug* to garnish. This dish pairs excellently with fresh, warm flatbread.

Tabeekh

Yemeni stewed vegetables

Serves 3

Tabeekh is a basic, comforting dish of stewed vegetables in a flavorful tomato gravy. It is simple, yet rich and grounding. For the tomato sauce, make your own pomarola ("marinara") or use a ready-made variety. The former is preferable for maintaining an authentic taste. Hawaij, the spice mix used in this recipe, is composed of freshly ground coriander, cumin, black pepper, cardamom, cinnamon, turmeric, and cloves.

INGREDIENTS

3	cloves of garlic, minced
2	chilies, chopped
1	onion, chopped
1	eggplant, chopped
1	tomato
1	small zucchini, chopped
1/2 cup	tomato sauce (not ketchup—more like a tomato purée or pasta sauce)
3	potatoes, chopped
1	tomato, chopped
1 tsp	*hawaij*
1/4 cup	oil
	salt and pepper, to taste

DIRECTIONS

1 Heat a large saucepan with the oil over medium-high. Sauté the onion, garlic, and chili for around 8 minutes, stirring occasionally to prevent burning.

2 Add the tomatoes and tomato sauce and cook for five more minutes. The oil should turn slightly red, indicating a rich flavor from the tomatoes.

3 Add the remaining vegetables and cook, covered, over medium-high for 20 minutes until the potatoes are soft and the liquid has been reduced. Stir occasionally to prevent burning.

4 Garnish with herbs and dried chilies, if desired. Serve hot with rice, bread, or *saltah* (p. 145).

Beverages

Yemeni Coffee

Yemen was the place where coffee was first cultivated commercially, and, before the introduction of coffee plants to other parts of the world, it was long the primary source of that most-coveted bean.

Yemeni Mountains. Photo by: Rod Waddington. Creative Commons Public License; https://flic.kr/p/gCXA8N

Mokha

The word *mocha* comes from the name of the Yemeni city Mokha, where coffee beans have been cultivated for centuries. Coffee (*qahwah* in Arabic) is known in the Islamic world as the "wine of the Prophet." Yemeni beans are known to score incredibly highly in quality ratings. They have a chocolate-y flavor, not dissimilar from the Ethiopian Harrar variety. The ancient varieties of coffee arabica grown in Yemen are found elsewhere perhaps only in Ethiopia, where they originate.

Coffee was originally shipped through the ancient port of Mokha and sold by, primarily, Egyptian traders throughout the world. When British colonial traders discovered this, they took the beans to the Caribbean and South America, where they promptly established slave colonies to cultivate and process the beans. This coffee would be sold primarily in the US and Europe, and the profits tended to be used to fund further colonial exploits.

Before coffee became so entwined in unethical colonial trade, however, it formed part of the fabric of Arab social life. Yemeni Mokha cultivation has not changed significantly in the past 500 years. The beans are grown on terraces of mountains above ancient stone villages. The site is spectacular.

Above: Arabic coffee harvest. Photo: WikiImages, Pixabay

Climate

Yemen is part of the Middle East desert biome—one of the largest biomes in the world. However, the country contains some significant subtropical microclimates. Mountainous elevation reaches three thousand feet above sea level at some points, and these mountains alter the course of the oceanic winds accompanying the South-West monsoon. Therefore, the climate in these high-biodiversity highlands is completely different to that of other areas in the country, which are dry and hot. One can find sparkling mountain streams, heavily mistified forests, and high-altitude agricultural terracing. The agricultural traditions here span two thousand years.

In the spring and summer, the trees blossom and the mountains turn a bright green. The coffee beans are picked when the weather turns cooler and the air dries out. The beans are sun-dried with the fruit still attached on the roofs of the stone houses above. The dried cherry husks, which are sometimes more valuable in Yemen than the beans, are removed with millstones. This technique of grinding the beans is one of the oldest technologies of coffee production. The result is coarse ground.

Custom

The husks of the dried coffee fruit are used to make a drink called *qishr*. The process of making it is both social and ritualistic. The ingredients are boiled and cooled three times in order to release the flavors. Along with the husks, *qishr* contains ginger and other spices. A version containing *qat* (or *khat*, a plant that is known to have stimulating properties) and red dates is offered to women shortly after childbirth due to its stimulating and tonic properties. The drink contains less caffeine than coffee but minimizes waste. It is customary to drink the *qishr* while chewing on the *qat* leaves. The natural chemicals released from the *qat* increase blood pressure and heart rate, much like coffee itself, although the practice is far older than that of drinking coffee. *Qishr* is often served as a digestive after meals. It is associated with the culture of hospitality as it is always offered to guests, and is frequently at the center of social gatherings.

Qishr

Yemeni spiced coffee

Qishr more closely resembles a deep, red tea than coffee. If you cannot find coffee husks, you may make the recipe with coffee. The flavor will be different, as will the effects on the body. Moreover, using coffee grounds is not "traditional," but substituting coffee for husks in qishr *is becoming more common. Qishr is customarily made in a pot called an* ibrik. *If you do not have one of these, you may use a regular, small saucepan. Qishr is a social drink and is meant to be enjoyed communally, so invite over some friends and family and serve them* qishr *in traditional Arabic tea glasses along with dates or sweets.*

INGREDIENTS

6 cups	water
1 cup	coffee husks *(qishr cascara) or . . .*
. . . 6 tsp	coffee
4 tsp	honey or sugar
1 tsp	ginger, grated

OPTIONAL

1	pod of cardamom
1/2 tsp	cinnamon
1/2 tsp	caraway seeds
1/4 cup	honey or sugar

DIRECTIONS

1   Lightly grind the coffee husks in a high-powered processor, mill, or grinder.

2   Combine all the ingredients and bring to boil in a saucepan over medium heat. Then, remove from heat and allow to cool.

3   When the bubbles have settled completely, return the pot to the stove and bring to boil again. Repeat this step one more time, so that the mixture has boiled and cooled three times.

4   Strain and serve in small, traditional Arabic coffee cups and enjoy with friends or family. Make sure to allow the grounds to settle to the bottom of the cups prior to serving.

pp. 152–153: Yemeni Highlands. Photo by: Rod Waddington, Flickr

Sana'a, with an elevation of 2250 meters (7,381 feet) above sea level, is the second highest capital city in Asia (after Timphu in Bhutan), and the seventh highest in the world. The city is located in Yemen's central highlands. More specifically, Sana'a is situated in a plateau between the Djebel Nogoum and the Djebel Ayban.

Left: View of Central Sanaa City Old Town. Photo: TravelPhotography

Next Spread: Manakah, Yemen. Photo: Davor Lovincic, iStock

pp. 160–161: Khartoum. Photo: Chicobarros, Pixabay

p. 162: Sunset view of Khartoum, Sudan. Photo: Ferozeea, iStockk

SUDAN AND SOUTH SUDAN

The states of Sudan and South Sudan were previously united as a single nation. South Sudan seceded from Sudan in 2011, forming an independent country. Prior to this, Sudan was the largest country in Africa (eight percent of Continental Africa and two percent of the world's total land). Naturally, both countries are extremely diverse—culturally, spiritually, linguistically, and socially. The decision to group both nations together is not intended to masquerade the diversity that exists within and across both nations, but simply to highlight the cultural and culinary contributions that they have shared for the past nine thousand years.

Sudanese culture places high value on sociality and community. Meals are often eaten on communal trays, on which various dishes are placed. As other parts of the Arab and Muslim worlds, hot, sweet tea is often consumed throughout the day. It accompanies breakfast, afternoon tea, the arrival of guests, and most other significant occasions. If coffee is preferred, it will be served in a tin pot known as a *jebena*. It is usually sweetened, and sometimes spiced with cinnamon or ginger.

Poetry

كُل شَيْءٍ

إطلق الرّيحَ من فَمِ الصيّادِ
إلى هيكلِ المُرَكَبِ ، من عُمْقِ الشراعِ
وفَكَّك الرُّبَطِ عن فَمِ النهرِ
أصرخ ْ
أيها الغريقُ
في اللُّجَجِ الدائرةِ

يبدأُ النهرُ من عاداته، ساكناً
يبدأُ الشاطئُ لَمُّ الشموسِ
من أفواه السمكِ الميِّتِ
يبدأُ طَهْوِ الظلالِ
من الرائحةِ، كنسَ الحصى

لكنَّ الهدوء—الريح—أصوات
الذين يركبون المقالع—لكنَّ السكونُ

يبحرونَ من ليلٍ بعيدٍ
يحفرونَ الماءَ بالصبر العتيدِ
وينظرونَ العَتْمَةَ

بينما أبحرتَ قُربَ الصباحِ
من محاياتٍ التي في صدرِهَا
أثبتَّ مَعنى
قادماً منها وتطلبُ الضفةَ—خضرةَ العمرِ وأوراق الهويةِ
بينما أخرى تؤجُّرُك البسيطةَ
بين عينيها
وتطلبُ صفوَ أوراق الكتابةِ—كلَّ شَيْءٍ !

Everything

Let the wind blow from a fisherman's mouth,
from the span of a sail to the shell of a boat,
unlocking the mouth of the river—
So, shout, drowning man, when you founder
in treacherous waters

At dawn, the river embarks in silence
Riverbanks glean suns from the scales of dead fish
Jostled by eddies, the aroma of flotsam and jetsam
bakes in the shade

Becalmed, a breeze freights the stillness
Sails lazily unfurl

They sail all night from afar,
ploughing the river with ritual persistence,
staring darkness straight in the eye

You set sail at dawn,
infused with the tincture of a heart
that had beached your whole life ashore
And yet, another beloved
is offering you heaven on earth in her glance,
demanding only the perfection of poetry—everything!

—Al-Saddiq Al-Raddi

Sudanese Cuisine

A culture is comprised of the accumulation of heritage. For a place like Sudan, with a rich migratory history, one can expect to locate innumerable influences within its historico-cultural repertoire. Local migration brought travelers from all over the continent; voyagers traversed vast land- and seascapes to dock in Sawakin or 'Aydhāb, the ancient ports. At one point, the Sawakin Port was the chief African Red Sea Port, as well as a major crossing for pilgrims en route to Mecca. Sudan's cuisines are therefore as diverse as its landscapes. These variations become pronounced as one traverses the country's vast terrain. The ports, however, were the first point of entry for most of what would later be incorporated into Sudanese culture.

Shifting our focus inland, central Sudan became known for its colorful and diverse customs. In addition to being a vibrant center for commercial activity, it was also where colonial influence was most perceptible. Red pepper, garlic, and other spices were brought to Sudan by Syrian traders under Ottoman rule. Dishes such as meatballs and sweet pastries were subsumed into the local diet(s). Evidently, the history of the Sudanese experience in the world is embedded in its internal cultures, written into their cuisines.

The north of Sudan has a history extending back thousands of years. This region's most popular food is a wheat crêpe, known as *gourrassa.* The ancient Nubians are thought to have been the first consumers of wheat, which remains a staple there today. The most popular dish in the eastern part of the country, *moukhbaza*, made from banana paste, speaks to a historical strand of Ethiopian influence. Dairy products, on the other hand, are fundamental components— *not just of diet, but of life itself*—in the Western regions, where cattle breeding is woven into the very fabric of social existence. Finally, in the south, where the environment is rich in streams and rivers, diets include a lot more fresh fish.

Mangoes, bananas, dates, and limes are the most widely cultivated fruit crops. Stews and vegetable dishes are flavored with dried onions, spices, and peanut butter, and accompanied by sorghum or millet *aseeda* (porridge), or *kissra*, a flatbread made of corn. Peanut butter is an archetypal flavor of Sudanese cuisine. In addition to being a thickener, it contributes a rich, nutty flavor that distinguishes Sudanese dishes—so much so that peanuts are known in Arabic as "ful Sudani," or "Sudani beans."

Regional flavors and local adaptations

In addition to having its own, unique cuisine(s), Sudan shares several dishes with the wider MENA (Middle East North African) region. The Sudanese version of falafel, called *tamiyya,* is sometimes made with broad beans, fava beans, black-eyed peas, or lentils. It is often prepared communally, which makes the process less labor intensive, faster, and more social. Sudanese and South Sudanese food can be quite complex, so working together and dividing the tasks among others allow for a more pleasant and grounding experience.

Porridge with peanuts, mangoes, and spices—a contemporary take on traditional Sudanese flavors.

The numbers

- Seven million people from South Sudan require emergency aid, including food, water, and medicine

- 2.5 million people have been displaced from South Sudan

- 60 percent of the displaced are children; 90 percent are women and children

- Many of the children fleeing the war between Sudan and South Sudan experience trauma, due to what they have witnessed

- More than six million South Sudanese people are food-insecure

- Uganda hosts more than one million South Sudanese refugees

Sudanese Sweet Potato and Peanut Stew

Lentils and vegetables stewed in a creamy, nutty stew

Serves 3

Peanuts play an important role in the Sudanese flavor profile. The nuts can be crushed, boiled, ground into a smooth butter, or fried golden-brown and added to an array of dishes, contributing both texture and flavor. The creamy butter serves as a rich, dairy-free thickener to sauces and stews, such as traditional spinach stew or this sweet potato stew, and also marks the Sudanese variation in regional dishes.

INGREDIENTS

1/2 cup	dry red lentils, rinsed
2	large white onions, diced
3	cloves of garlic, minced
1 tsp	turmeric
1/2 tsp	paprika
1 tsp	cumin
1/2 tsp	chili powder
1/2 cup	peanuts
1 cube	vegetable bouillon
3 T	tomato paste
2	sweet potatoes
2 T	creamy peanut butter
1-inch	piece of ginger, minced
1 cup	raw kale or spinach, chopped finely
	salt and pepper, to taste
	olive oil

DIRECTIONS

1   Bring the lentils to boil in a saucepan of water. Turn to simmer and leave, covered, until lentils are tender. Drain.

2   Sauté onions and garlic in olive oil with turmeric, paprika, cumin, chili powder, and peanuts in a stockpot.

3   When the onions are soft, add the lentils, sweet potatoes, peanut butter, salt, pepper, ginger, tomato paste, bouillon, and 1 liter of water. Cook on high until boiling, mixing to prevent the bottom from burning.

4   Once boiling, turn the heat to medium-low and leave, covered, for 30 minutes, stirring occasionally. The potatoes should be soft and succulent. If desired, you may use an immersion blender for a few pulses to purée some of the stew.

5   Add kale a few minutes before serving. Serve over rice and garnish with some chopped coriander and more peanuts.

Bread and Grain

Porridge, or *aseeda*, is a staple in the Sudanese diet—and not only for breakfast. Porridge made from wheat, finger millet, sorghum, or corn flour may be served alongside stews or vegetable dishes. As in Ethiopia and Eritrea, fermented flatbreads are popular in Sudan. Crêpes made from sorghum (*kissra*) or wheat flour (*gourrassa*) are common accompaniments to meals.

Ahbab M.

"Ahbab Moustapha, a 28-year-old baker of the camp, has one wife and two children. He was working in a bakery in Sudan, in El Geneina, the capital of West Darfur State.

I start my work at 1.30 in the morning and finish it at 8.30 a.m. with the last bake. Then I rest until 11 a.m. and see how the day turns out. Then I buy the input for the next day's bakes and have my lunch. Around 3 or 6 p.m., I clean my oven. I work every day, because people eat bread every day. I sell one of the bread for 50 CFA (10 US cents). My stockists buy 100 pieces for 4500 CFA and make a 5 CFA profit on a bread. There are around ten bakers in all of the camp. My team is composed of three assistants to make the bread and two sellers who sell even in Goz Beida [the Chadian city located four kilometers from the camp]. I will go back to Sudan when everyone will go back. I will start a new life and will have my own business, a bakery in Hashaba, near Bayda.

Top: A baker in Djabal camp in east Chad. Photo: Frederic Noy, UNHCR. Creative Commons Public License. This photo has been edited.

Bottom: A baker in El Fashar, North Darfur, Sudan. Photo: Albert Gonzalez Farran, UNAMID, Creative Commons Public License, https://flic.kr/p/fG8LDK. This photo has been edited.

ETHIOPIA AND ERITREA

Habesha is a word that Ethiopian and Eritrean people sometimes use to identify themselves. The word is designed not to wash over differences, but to unite two peoples and celebrate the aspects of their cultures that are common to both. The term is not all-encompassing, and includes the following five linguisitic groups: Tigre, Tigrinya, Gurage, Amharic, and Harrari.

Eritreans and Ethiopians have a shared history that extends back more than three thousand years, but Eritrea seceded from Ethiopia in 1991. The region is extremely diverse, with many different languages, tribes, and ethnic groups. Notwithstanding the differences in Eritrean and Ethiopian demographics, traditions, and culture, many of the traditional dishes cannot be attributed to one or the other, since they have long been prevalent in both places. In these cases, I have referred to them as *Habeshi* dishes or traditions.

My decision to group them together is by no means meant to erase the differences and nuances that certainly exist both between and within them, nor to marginalize any others who do not identify with the terms. My aim is merely to explore the many cultural contributions that Ethiopian and Eritrean peoples have historically shared, and continue to share today.

Previous Page: Blue Nile Falls, Ethiopia. Photo: alekosa, Adobe Stock

This page: Religious ceremony (St. George's Day). Photo: Alex, Adobe Stock

Religion

Both nations are home to all Abrahamic religions, as well as native African ones. Most of Ethiopian and Eritrean history has been characterized by the peaceful coexistence of religious groups, most of which are extremely old. Both the Muslim and Jewish communities remained under the governance of the Emperor, who was always Orthodox Christian, the Protector of the Church, and officiated as the head of the Church in a crowning ceremony. Despite this, members of other religions have experienced more freedom to practice and dress according to their religions than has been the case in other countries.

Christianity

Ethiopia has one of the oldest Christian populations in the world. Orthodox Christianity is the official state religion in Ethiopia, where it has played a significant role in politics. An attempt by the Crown to mass-convert the population to Christianity in the nineteenth century was resisted by followers of other faiths, as evidenced by the persistence of these communities today. Conversely, religion has been somewhat less of a political force in Eritrea. Other religions may therefore have a greater presence there due to the absence of a dominant public religion.

Islam

Ethiopia holds a very important place in Islamic history. Islam is the second most populous religion, and the Muslim population is extremely ancient. The first Muslim community in Mecca faced immense persecution from the Quraysh in the seventh century. Many fled to Axum, an Ethiopian city that had accepted Islam early on, and where they would "find a king who does not wrong anyone." King Negus, or al-Najashi, was known as a just ruler who respected religious freedom. This migration was known as the First Hijra, or "flight." However, the community remained small as the spread of the religion took place gradually and peacefully.

Judaism

The *Beta Israel* Jewish community of Ethiopia has existed for at least 1500 years. It is believed that many Jewish peoples arrived from around the region between the first and sixth centuries CE. While Ethiopian Jews have been prominent members of Ethiopian society, they often lived by their own religious laws under the immediate guidance of Jewish leaders. They maintain their own unique religious customs and practices, which can be quite different from those of other Jewish communities around the world. An order of Ethiopian Jewish monks was founded in the fifteenth century to enhance the community's religious identity, which introduced new prayers, as well as other adaptations to religious activities.

Injera

Injera is perhaps the most recognizable symbol of Habeshi cuisines. The spongy flatbread is made from *teff*—widely considered one of the most nutritious grains. Having originated in Ethiopia and Eritrea between 4000 and 1000 BCE, *teff* was one of the earliest domesticated plants in the world. Naturally gluten-free, it is rich in calcium, fiber, protein, a high concentration of amino acids, and many anti-oxidants. Preparation of *injera* is quite labor-intensive. The *teff* grains are stone-ground into flour. The flour is then fermented in water for several days, at which point it is made into a batter and poured on a clay plate, a *mitad*, and cooked on one side like a large crêpe or dosa. The freshly cooked flatbreads are then rolled into cylinders and placed in a basket, called a *mesab*. Alternatively, a round of *injera* can be laid flat on a large dish and topped with a variety of stews and vegetable dishes. The spongy bread absorbs all the flavors of the stews, making it the perfect utensil. *Fitfi* is another dish composed of vegetables, legumes, and seeds in a hot broth with pieces of *injera* that soak up all the flavor.

Sharing is an important aspect of Habeshi culture(s). According to custom, once a dish is placed on the table, no one rises until all are done and the tray is removed. Food is sacred, and the enjoyment of it should not be rushed. It is also eaten with the hands, which allows the consumer to be present, intentional, and connected in the act of eating.

Vegan food and the "Veggie Combo"

The "veggie combo" (*nai tsom migbi* or *yetsom beyanetu* in Tigrinya and Amharic, respectively), pictured left, has long been present on Habeshi tables. Samplings of vibrant, vegetable-filled dishes are served atop injera. This way of eating facilitates community and allows people to enjoy a wide variety of flavors and nutrients. The veggie platter is known vernacularly as "fasting food" because it complies with Orthodox Christian fasting traditions, which prescribe that its adherants abstain from eating meat and other animal products for as much as two-thirds of the year. In both Ethiopia and Eritrea, fasting is a constituent element of social and religious life. The variety in each serving, which often includes *berbere*-spiced lentil stew and sautéed greens, ensures that those who fast adequately meet their micro- and macro-nutrient requirements.

The national dish is a chicken stew cooked with *berbere*, called *doro wat*. However, there is a version of this dish, which is Orthodox fasting–compliant, known as *shimbera asa wot*, or literally "chickpea fish stew," whose primary protein is a dumpling made of chickpea flour, which is first baked separately and then added to the stew to absorb all the flavors. Sometimes the dumplings are molded to evoke fish, with little fins. Hard-boiled eggs are substituted with egg-shaped potatoes, and together with the rich flavor of the *berbere*, the result is a dish that resembles *doro wat* in both appearance and piquancy.

Colonialism

Eritrea was colonized by Italy in the late nineteenth century, and remained under colonial rule for decades. British forces also occupied both nations for periods during those decades. Even in the moment of decolonization, there was extensive foreign intervention due to the strategic position Eritrea occupied among Red Sea nations. In the Cold War, the politics of religious divides became a strategic weapon for Superpower states. This is just one of many examples in which internal disputes became exploited for international power struggles.

Some remnants of Italian food culture remained even after independence. It is more noticeable in Eritrea, where the colonial experience was longer and more severe. Dessert was not a typical element of Ethiopian culinary habits, but Italian sweets such as Tiramisu and chocolate mousse have become some of the go-to options. As the birthplace of coffee, Ethiopia clearly affected the culinary repertoires of European nations as well. Ethiopian cakes and pastries are typically dairy-free, in order to comply with the conventions of Orthodox-Christian fasting.

Atakilt Wat

Ethiopian cabbage and potato stir fry

Serves 6

....

This naturally vegan dish is a common addition to a typical Ethiopian beyanetu. *Traditionally, you would use an Ethiopian* mitmita *spice mix, but since that might be difficult to find, this recipe calls for spices that can be easily found in most pantries. Tear off a piece of injera with your right hand and use it as a scoop to hold the* atakilt wat. *You will be participating in a way of eating that dates back over three thousand years. If you'd like, you may add finely chopped collard greens.*

....

INGREDIENTS

1/4 cup	canola oil
1 T	turmeric
1 tsp	curry powder
1 tsp	paprika
1/2 tsp	chili powder
2	cloves of garlic, minced
2/3-inch	piece of ginger, grated
1–2 T	tomato paste
1/2 head	green cabbage, chopped
2	large onions, diced
3	carrots
5	large, waxy potatoes (e.g. Yukon Gold)
	salt and pepper, to taste

DIRECTIONS

1   Wash and peel the carrots and potatoes. Then, chop them into 1-inch chunks.

2   In a large pot, heat the oil on high. Add the turmeric, curry powder, paprika, chili powder, and garlic. Tempering the spices causes the fragrances to release in the most flavorful way.

3   Add the ginger and onion. Sauté for 10 minutes, stirring occasionally to prevent burning.

4   Incorporate the remaining ingredients and cook, covered, on low heat for 25 minutes. Make sure to stir the pot every few minutes. When it is ready, the vegetables should be succulent, but not mushy.

5   Sprinkle with salt and serve with rice or injera.

Berbere Spice Mix

Berbere, *meaning "hot" in Amharic, is a spice blend used in many Ethiopian and Eritrean dishes. The spices are ground and roasted until fragrant—the deep, red hue contributing a warm color to the dishes that contain it. While berbere is traditionally spicy, feel free to adapt the proportion of chili to paprika according to your taste. As always, the best flavor results from grinding the spices by hand with a pestle and mortar, but you may use a food processor or blender if this is not available to you. If you decide to go for the latter option, use the "pulse" option to grind the spices in short bursts.*

INGREDIENTS

2 tsp	coriander seeds
1/2 tsp	black peppercorns
1/2 tsp	fenugreek seeds
1/2 tsp	nigella seeds
5	pods of cardamom (husks removed)
4	cloves of garlic
1/2 cup	dried onion flakes
5	dried chilies
3 T	paprika
2 tsp	salt
1/2 tsp	cinnamon, ground
1 tsp	ginger, ground
1/2 tsp	nutmeg, ground
1/4 tsp	allspice, ground
1/4 tsp	*ajwain* seeds
optional: 1 T	basil, dried

DIRECTIONS

1 Gently toast the coriander, fenugreek, peppercorns, cardamom, garlic, and allspice over medium heat in a non-stick pan—about 3–5 minutes.

2 Remove from heat and allow to cool. Then, grind or blend the spice mix with the dried onions and chilies until fine.

3 Mix in the remaining ingredients. Use immediately or store in an airtight container.

Ethiopian Coffee

Coffee is a mainstay of Ethiopian and Eritrean culture. Ethiopia is the birthplace of the coffee bean, and continues to be a source for some of the best coffee in the world. Macchiatos made with local sunflower milk came into vogue in the twentieth century—the dairy-free milk being compliant with Orthodox fasting dicta.

The traditional function of coffee exceeds the role of a "morning caffeine fix." It is a ceremony that extends far back in history. The daily ritual signifies a time of communion, where men or women get together and discuss the day's happenings over cups of organic, freshly ground coffee (usually with popcorn). The coffee ceremony is a time for respect: for one's blessings, one's elders, and the bounty of the earth.

The scent of burning incense and raw green beans roasting over a charcoal brazier in a *menkeskesh* envelops the room and intoxicates the senses. The entire process is sensuous. The beans are poured on a woven mat to cool. As I watch, the small pot is thrust in front of my nose so I may catch a whiff of the mesmerizing aroma. I can barely wait.

The beans are then stone-ground with a pestle and mortar into a grain whose size falls somewhere between espresso and drip coffee. The grounds are brewed in an earthenware pot, called a *jebena*. The form of the *jebena* differs in Ethiopia and Eritrea, as well as across families and regions, but in most cases it has a round bottom and sits in a kind of holder. A modest amount of water is poured into it to brew, and the pot will be re-heated over the fire if needed. When it is ready, the coffee is poured into small cups and drunk black. Its flavor is smooth and rich. If seconds are wanted, which will certainly be the case, more water can be added and the pot heated once more.

p. 190: Ethiopian pilgrim at Lalibela church, Ethiopia. Photo: Rafal Cichawa, Alamy

p. 191: Woman's hand pouring coffee for traditional Ethiopian coffee ceremony. Photo: Wollwerth Imagery, Adobe Stock

pp. 194–195: Palmyra. Photo: andrelambo, Pixabay

pp. 196–197: Al-Khalidieh. Photo: Freedom House, Flickr

SYRIA

Syria has a rich culture and history that dates back eight thousand years. Before the war, Syrian citizens enjoyed free healthcare and education, and a fast-growing economy.

During the Arab Spring in 2011, peaceful demonstrations were met with increasing and disproportionate violence by government forces. The clashes escalated quickly, with students experiencing harsh crackdowns. Before long, mercenaries started arriving from all over the world to join the conflict on all sides. The effects of the violence reached all segments of the Syrian population, including its youngest and most vulnerable.

Over half the population (more than 12 million people) have been killed or forced to flee their homes.

Ninety-five percent of Syrian refugees are hosted in Turkey, Lebanon, Jordan, Iraq, and Egypt. In addition, millions are internally displaced—and running out of basic resources fast.

Destroyed Homs centre, Syria. Photo: Goran Safarek

The numbers

- 13.1 million people in Syria require urgent humanitarian assistance. Over 25 percent are located in areas with little access to aid.

- An estimated 470,000 people have been killed since the war began, including around 55,000 children.

- 95 percent of people in Syria do not have access to proper healthcare.

- 70 percent of people in Syria do not have access to a clean water supply.

- More than two million Syrian children are out of school (UNICEF 2017).

- Nearly six million Syrians have fled as refugees.

- 90 percent of Syrian refugees are being hosted in the Middle East, compared with just two percent in Europe.

- Only 8 percent of Syrian refugees live in registered camps.

Left: Children playing in the ruins of Aleppo. Photo: IHH International Humanitarian Relief Foundation. Creative Commons Public License, https://flic.kr/p/mC9de1. This photo has been edited.

The influence or prevalence of Middle Eastern food on Europe has always been contingent on circumstance—on war; on trade; on seasonality; and not least of all, on politics.

The cuisines in these areas are known for their uses of affective aromatics and sensuous spices. Therefore, developments in external factors such as Christian theology contributed to the changing significance of certain foods. Puritanism and Calvinism, for instance, advocated for the suppression of pleasure and the denial of sensuality.

In the Middle Ages, when trade between the East and West was flourishing, ships of wheat, rice, nuts, dried fruit, sugar (which was new to Europe), rosewater, tahini, pomegranate syrup, tamarind, saffron, mastic, and orange-blossom water found their way to European epicures. These trade routes encouraged innovation and inspiration, and enabled people from all over the world to look at new ways of doing things.

"In Syria,

nobody can sit at a table without *khubz* (خبز)—the Arabic word for bread. It is at the core of all our meals. In fact, its significance transcends culture and country: it's a key pillar of Syrian society. We use thin flatbread to eat almost everything. There is a technique to it though, so if you come to my pop-ups you can put your *khubz*-scooping skills to the test."

—**Mohammed**, founder of @Mos_eggs, London

Life is a struggle for Syrian refugees in Lebanon, who have little to no economic rights or resources. There are few refugee camps, and those that exist primarily harbor the long-standing Palestinian refugee community, which has been in exile for decades, and who do not fare much better. Consequently, the majority of Syrian refugees in Lebanon live below the poverty line, sharing cramped living spaces with other destitute refugee families. They survive on informal work, or by selling goods and services at below-market prices.

Dawood Basha

Syrian meatballs with yogurt and tomato sauces

Serves 3

If it wasn't clear from the title (pasha was a designation given to high ranking Ottoman officials), this dish came to the Arab World via the Ottoman Empire. Legend goes that it was created for a certain Dawood Pasha, who ruled over Iraq and Lebanon. In this version, I've used a dairy-free yogurt and plant-based "meatballs."

INGREDIENTS—MEATBALLS

2 1/2 cups	ground beef vegan equivalent
2	large onions, diced
2	cloves of garlic, minced
1 tsp	salt
1/2 tsp	smoked paprika
1/4 cup	tamari or soy sauce (if using vegetarian mince)
1 tsp	allspice
1 tsp	dried mint
1/2 tsp	cinnamon

TOMATO SAUCE

1 1/2	onions, diced
1	clove of garlic, minced
3	tomatoes, chopped
3	potatoes, chopped
2	capsicum peppers, chopped
3 cups	water
3 T	tomato paste
pinch	salt

DIRECTIONS

1 Mix all of the meatball ingredients, either in a food processor or by hand. Then, roll the mixture into meatballs.

2 Heat some oil in a frying pan. When the oil is sufficiently hot, add the meatballs and fry on medium-high until browned and slightly crispy on the outside. Make sure they are cooked on all sides, resulting in a meatball that has some texture but is still juicy and tender inside.

3 For the tomato sauce, sauté the onions and garlic with some olive oil in a saucepan until they become semi-translucent.

4 Add the rest of the sauce ingredients. Cover and cook on medium heat for 20–25 minutes, until the potatoes are tender. If the sauce is too watery, cook uncovered for a further 10 minutes.

TO ASSEMBLE

1 Place the meatballs atop a bed of tomato sauce. Cover them with more tomato sauce. Meanwhile, fry the oil, garlic and paprika on medium-high for 3 minutes.

2 Pour the plain yogurt over the meatballs, followed by the garlic oil. Garnish with chopped herbs and toasted pine nuts. Serve with rice and *Shirazi* salad.

GARNISH

1 cup	dairy-free yogurt equivalent (e.g., cashew)
2 T	neutral oil
1	clove of garlic, minced
handful	pine nuts
1/4 cup	chopped coriander and/ or mint

Iraq

Iraq has a long and illustrious history. It was the seat of the Abbasid Empire from the eighth century CE; and was, at various times, ruled by the Mongols, the Ottomans, and the British. Its remarkable splendor came with some unfortunate circumstances, since Iraqi lands contained vast reserves of vital resources.

It has seen incredible heights, as well as tragic lows. The Islamic Golden Age was a period of immense prosperity situated among an abundant and dynamic intellectual environment. It commenced with the founding of the House of Wisdom in Baghdad, by Caliph Harun al-Rashid—and lasted some centuries. Philosophers, doctors, lawyers, theologians, and all manner of thinkers gathered from all over the world to discuss important topics in the newly established space. Many were recruited from among prominent Jewish, Hindu, Muslim, and Christian scholars, and a lively spirit of collaboration existed within the institution. These scholars also translated important texts, such as the works of Aristotle, from Greek into Arabic in order to be made available to the rest of the Arab world. This period of time produced great scientists (Persian and Arabic), including Al-Razi, the Persian scientist who practiced medicine and ran the hospital in Baghdad; Ibn Sina (Avicenna), from eleventh-century Baghdad, who wrote the *Canon of Medicine*; and Ibn Rushd (Averroes), the famed twelfth-century philosopher and astronomer.

In more recent history, the heart of Iraq has lived through centuries of colonial occupation, a dictatorship, and two devastating wars. All of these factors have influenced the ability of art and culture to prosper. After the invasion in 2003, more than 170,000 artifacts were stolen from the National Museum. Such changes become transcribed into food as well, as people and goods experience changes in their movements around the world.

The numbers

- More than 11 million Iraqis are in need of urgent humanitarian assistance.

- More than 2.6 million Iraqis have been forced to flee their homes, while 3.5 million have been displaced internally.

- Two million Iraqi refugees were hosted by Syria after the US invasion. Conversely, 250,000 Syrian refugees are now being hosted in Iraq.

- More than 86,000 Iraqis arrived on the shores of Greece in 2015 alone. Even though they've escaped the clutches of the Islamic State, living conditions in Greece have been difficult, plagued by famine, illness, and harsh weather conditions.

Left: Child on a bicycle. Photo: Isakarakus, Pixabay

Next spread: Iraqi children. Photo: Bluemix, Pixabay XX

The War Economy

Following the imposition of sanctions, the economic situation became considerably worse, with Iraq's national income falling from 13,863 million dinar to 3,548 million dinar, a drop of almost 75 percent (Niblock 2001, 173) in the first year. Or, as Garfield (1999, 12) points out, during "the first eight years of the embargo, Iraq estimates that it lost U.S.$120 bn [billion] in foreign exchange earnings" but received only $1 billion in humanitarian donations. Recent figures suggest that per capita income is now about U.S.$255 per household (UNDP 2005, 138), less than it was in 1980, few other countries (particularly with oil resources) are facing a level of income per household lower than it was more than twenty-five years ago. —**Jennifer Olmsted**, "Globalization Denied: Gender and Poverty in Iraq and Palestine" (p. 179)

Hundreds of thousands of children lost their lives as a result of economic sanctions. While medication was technically excluded from the sanctions, the international response to Iraqi medical import requests was typically very slow. In addition, many healthcare practitioners fled the country during the war, making it difficult to train new personnel. Throughout the years, the medical equipment became old and sometimes defective. Other medical problems resulted from the struggle other sectors outside of healthcare faced to survive. For instance, the sanitation sector was "unable to maintain a water delivery system after sanctions were imposed, leading to a rapid drop in the availability of clean water, which in turn was linked to increased disease and death." (Olmsted, 180)

In 1990, 90 percent of Iraqis were receiving safe drinking water. By 1996, 25 percent of water was contaminated and the amount of water available per capita had declined by 40 percent. Sixty-seven percent of rural households were unable to access safe sources at time of study, and 40 percent of urban households were unable to access safe sources.

Other countries that have faced UN sanctions include: Southern Rhodesia, South Africa, Yugoslavia, Somalia, Libya, Liberia, Haiti, Angola, Rwanda, Sierra Leone, and the Sudan (Garfield, 1999). In addition, the US has laid embargoes on Iran and Cuba.

Punitive sanctions and the total devastation of infrastructure have economically imprisoned the Iraqi people. The ability of a culture (and its cuisines) to survive depends on the ability of its people to carry it. It will be imperative, for the sake of humanity, that we ensure the freedom and safety of the Iraqi people and their brethren all over the world, living under the same conditions. We all benefit from the remarkable diversity of this planet.

Left: Destroyed and abandoned building. Photo: Maxim-Khassanov, iStock

p. 218: Zakho, Kurdistan, Iraq. Photo: Aram Sabah, Unsplash

p. 219: Woman praying. Photo: Ghadeer, Unsplash

Influences on Iraqi Food

"Iraq's cuisine reflects its topographical and ethnic diversity. Located in the western corner of Asia, Iraq was first named Mesopotamia (land between two rivers), as both the Tigris and Euphrates rivers run through it. The north is partially mountainous, and mostly inhabited by the Kurds and other ethnic minorities. The rest of the country is made up of a fertile plain populated mostly by Arabs, and a western desert inhabited by nomadic Bedouins. Iraqis enjoy a refined cuisine with roots in over five thousand years of documented history from Mesopotamian times, through the golden medieval era when Baghdad ruled the Arabo-Islamic world, on to the present."—**Nawal Nasrallah**, ed. Karen Christensen (pp. 102–106)

Topography

According to scholars, Iraq's topography is its most significant influence—more so than religion or ethnicity (Nasrallah, Christensen). "The northern region is where the wheat-based dishes abound, such as those cooked with bulgur (cracked wheat). . . . Dishes from this region, with its verdant pastures, tend to include more yogurt than elsewhere in the country. In the Central and Southern regions, non-wheat grains such as rice and barley are staples due to climatic conditions. These regions are dependent on the Tigris and Euphrates rivers" (see pp. 102, 274).

Trade

The Abbasid Caliphate was a time of great prosperity for the region known presently as Iraq. Baghdad was a cosmopolitan metropolis, located at the intersection of East and West—Persia, Greece, and Rome (Nasrallah, Christensen). The cuisine in the capital was renowned for its sophistication, and it was written about extensively by travelers. The Silk Road spice trade and the newly available ingredients from the "New World" cooperated to drive innovation in "traditional" cuisine. Stews, for instance, have been a linchpin of Iraqi kitchens for millennia. However, the introduction of tomatoes, from Colombia, altered the way they were made. They began to take the place of other ingredients (e.g. pomegranate syrup), and few stews remain today that do not feature tomatoes. The rise of the sugar industry led to the alterations in existing dessert recipes as well as the creation of new ones—heretofore limited to natural, available sweeteners such as honey and date syrup. Iraqi food is not known to be spicy, but the city of Basra, in the south, is an exception. This city has had a long mercantile history with India. The two primary spice mixes in Iraqi cuisine are *baharat* and *bahar asfar*.

Iraqi Dates

The *date* (tamar, تمر) is the most important fruit in Iraq, as it is for many Middle Eastern countries. The date palm is the "national tree" of Iraq, and its fruit gave it the epithet of "tree of life." There are hundreds of varieties of dates, which vary both across and within countries. Dates were a major source of sustenance for Bedouin populations all over the Gulf, containing abundant nutrients and being adaptable to harsh climates. The date also has significance in Islam, as a "holy fruit," as well as the ideal fast-breaker during Ramadan.

In addition to being eaten fresh, date syrup (*dibis*) is also used in a wide variety of dishes (Baklava, p. 311; Bulgur Salad, p. 279; *Qatayef Thuraya*, p. 315; *Qorma-e-Zardaloo*, p. 137; and *Dolmeh Felfel*, p. 305), and, as a paste, features in *Kleicha*, the national cookie of Iraq (p. 321).

Iraq used to be the world's largest producer of dates. Before the Iran–Iraq war, Iraq had 30 million date palms and produced one million metric tons of dates every year. The industry was neglected during and after the war, so that yearly production fell to 40 percent of its original output, while the number of date palms was reduced by half. The production of dates also requires agile young people to scale the trees, though increasingly more youths are opting for jobs in the public and civic sectors. As of the time of writing, the Ministry of Agriculture has laid out an $US80-million plan to rebuild the date palm inventory to up to 40 million trees in the next decade. The plan also lays out strategies to transition to more marketable varieties, since 90 percent of Iraqi date production was of a single variety, the Zehdi. Agriculture currently contributes 10.2 percent to national GDP, with the bulk of the remainder coming from oil.

Left: Date palm. Photo: Simon, Pixabay

Mtabbaq Tofu over Yellow Rice

Serves 4

Fish has been a part of the Iraqi diet for millennia. However, today 75 percent of the world's fisheries have been destroyed due to overfishing. Moreover, as the oceans become more polluted, fish accumulate ever-more toxic materials and heavy metals, such as mercury, in their bodies. This is incredibly dangerous for both human and sea life. We've taken a traditional Iraqi recipe and subbed the fish for firm tofu. Forget everything you know about tofu and try this dish. It's delicious, light, and ocean-friendly!

INGREDIENTS

YELLOW RICE—*serves 4*

1 tsp	turmeric
3 T	neutral oil
2 cups	dry basmati rice, soaked for 20 minutes and rinsed
4 cups	water
1 tsp	salt
5	pods of cardamom, whole
2	bay leaves
1-inch	cinnamon stick

ONION TOPPING

1	large white onion, diced
1 tsp	curry powder
1 tsp	turmeric
2	cloves of garlic
handful	raisins
handful	cranberries or barberries
handful	chopped coriander

TOFU and SAUCE

1/2 cup	smooth mustard
1/2 cup	agave, honey, or date syrup
1/3 cup	tamari or soy sauce
1 tsp	smoked paprika
1 tsp	ground thyme
1 block	firm tofu, drained and pressed (preferably for 2+ hours).

DIRECTIONS

1. Add all rice ingredients to a large, non-stick pot. Mix, cover and cook on medium-high for 8 minutes.

2. Turn heat to low and simmer for 20–25 minutes, covered. Make sure not to let the steam out or your rice will be dry.

3. When the rice is cooked, use a fork to fluff the rice by folding it carefully. This allows air to circulate and prevents the bottom half from becoming too dense.

4. Mix all ingredients for the tofu sauce (except the block of tofu) until combined.

(cont'd on next page)

5   Slice the block of tofu into fillets of about 3x4x1 inches. Cover with paper towels or cloths to drain any excess water. You can place the fillets in a flat dish and marinate with some of the sauce.

6   Meanwhile, heat some oil in a medium-sized frying pan. Fry the onions, curry powder, turmeric, and garlic until the onions become translucent. Add the dried fruit and herbs and cook for another 4–5 minutes.

7   Heat 2–4 T canola oil in another pan. Gently place the tofu fillets in the sizzling-hot oil and fry on medium-high until crispy. If you like smoky flavors, you can ever-so-slightly char the tofu.

8   Serve as pictured with some vegan raita.

SOMALIA

Somalia is the easternmost country of Africa, bordering Djibouti, Kenya, Yemen, Ethiopia, and the Indian Ocean. Somalia extends from south of the equator to the Gulf of Aden and therefore occupies an important geopolitical position as a trading hub connecting Africa, Asia, and the Middle East. It has the longest coastline in Africa, connecting to both the Red Sea and the Indian Ocean, and primarily consists of plateaus, plains, and highlands.

Like all refugee groups, Somalis are resourceful and resilient. Today, over two million people are internally displaced, while around 900,000 Somali refugees live in the surrounding areas (mostly Kenya, Yemen, and Ethiopia). Most began fleeing during the civil war and famine of 1991.

The effects of climate change are being widely felt in the country, which has seen an increase in droughts in recent years. Between November 2016 and March 2017, more than 615,000 people were displaced by drought. This further exacerbates food insecurity, with over six million people in need of humanitarian aid and almost one million children severely or acutely malnourished. (UNHCR).

We would like to thank Shukri Abdikarim and Abderazzaq Noor (*www.somalikitchen*) for their contributions to this book. Their website is a fantastic resource for anyone wishing to learn more about the culture, food, and recipes of Somalia and her communities in exile.

Somalia is rich in fruit, grains, and legumes—and the culinary traditions reflect this. Dates, apples, mangos, guava, oranges, grapes, pears, and bananas grow well, and it is commonly said that a meal is not complete without a banana. The banana is sliced, and then eaten with rice, pasta, or any other grain. Somali food gains its splendor not through the overprocessing of enriched ingredients, but through the careful preparation of each component. The subtle flavors of individual vegetables and grains are coaxed through their delicate cooperation with the others. Oils are slowly infused with spices and seeds. Cardamom, ginger, coriander, nutmeg, and cinnamon-infused blends bubble around pieces of chopped onion, which caramelizes as they grow tender. This fragrant mix then coats the grains of uncooked rice, like gold paint. Finally, the entire thing is cooked with water or vegetable stock until the grains have softened and swollen, amounting to a perfectly fluffiy, spiced rice.

The Somali *anjera* is similar to the *injera* of Eritrea and Ethiopia, though sometimes corn flour or sorghum flour is added to the *teff*. *Anjera* with sweet tea is a common breakfast food, especially for children. A sauce can be made from tea, butter, and sugar.

Meals are also family occasions. Lunch is typically the largest meal of the day. It would include meat and/or a variety of vegetables, beans, fresh banana, and salad, dressed around grain. The most popular are rice, pasta, and wheat breads, such as roti or chapathi.

Corn is a big part of Somali cultural life. Every autumn, men, women, and children come together to partake in the harvesting process. From there, the corn may be roasted, boiled, or ground into a polenta.

pp. 228–229: Giraffe. Photo: JamesDeMers, Pixabay

pp. 230–231: Wheat fields. Photo: Kimmy Williams, Unsplash

p. 232: Man at prayer. Photo: FS-stock, Adobe Stock

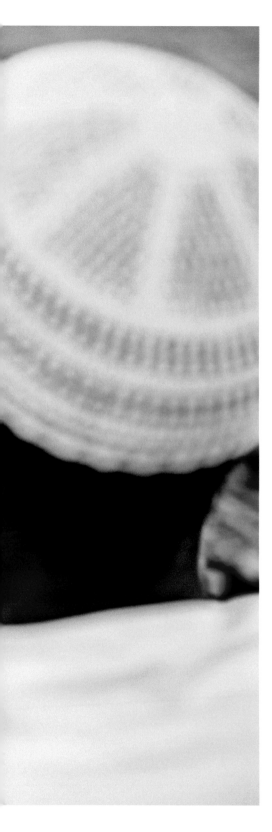

Cultural influences on food

Somali food is a rich mélange of flavors, spices, and ingredients, reflecting its centrality—both geographically and commercially—to important trading routes. The cuisine unmasks both spoken and untold histories, from the Horn of Africa to the East and beyond. Somalis belong to the Cushitic indigenous group. The name *Somalia* refers to the nomadic history of Somali people.

Trade

Somalia is located on the Indian Ocean and the Gulf of Aden, making it an important trading hub. The ancient coast townships of Mogadishu (the current capital), Kismayo, Marca, and Barawa were built up by the Arab and Persian traders, who brought spices, such as cumin, chili, coriander, cloves, and garlic, as well as rice. Flatbreads such as paratha, or *sabaayad* in Somali, can be traced to Indian merchants, while other contributions may be detected from Pakistan, Yemen, and other African cultures. These exchanges were by no means one-way: Somalis established many new culinary traditions in the places they migrated to as well—be it in Kenya, Uganda, Tanzania, the United Arab Emirates, Yemen, Oman, or Egypt.

Colonialism

Somalia was a powerful center of commerce and wealth before it became fragmented under European colonial rule. Periods of military occupation lasted until 1969, when General Mohamed Siad Barre led a coup for independence. The country was dissected into three parts: the French North, the Central "red coast," or British; and the South, Italian. The passing down of recipes facilitates this flexibility, since they largely escaped the rigidity of being written into code. Under Italian influence, pasta and tomato sauce were adopted into the local repertoire, and are featured in a famous dish called "Federation," which contains rice layered with vegetables and pasta, seasoned with tomatoes and spices. Similarly, the English puddings and French pastries bespeak Western European influence.

Religion

The majority of Somalis practice Islam. Therefore, pork and alcohol are not traditional elements in the cuisine. During Ramadan, Somalis fast from eating and drinking from dusk until dawn. This practice excludes pregnant, breastfeeding, and menstruating women, children, and those who are ill or traveling, as is Islamic custom. However, Ramadan is not the only time where Somalis may fast. Fasting has been used as a tool by all spiritual traditions.

The numbers

- 4.7 million people (40 percent of the population) in Somalia require humanitarian assistance.

- 950,000 people in Somalia suffer severe food insecurity. 300,000 children under five are suffering malnutrition.

- The Somali refugee crisis has lasted three decades. There are now third-generation Somali refugees (UNHCR).

- One million Somalis have sought refuge in neighboring countries.

- 260,000 people have died as a result of drought in Somalia in the last decade, which has affected access to water, food, and healthcare.

- Hundreds of Somalis died trying to cross the Mediterranean in 2016.

- Somalis, along with Iranians, Syrians, Yemenis, Venezuelans, North Koreans, and Libyans, were banned from entering the US due to the 2017 Travel Ban.

Mango Curry

Serves 4

Mango, or ambe, *adds a delicate sweetness to the dish, softening the spices. When selecting the mango for this recipe, it should be soft to squeeze, but not rotten. As the mango ripens, it becomes sweeter and more flavorful. It should have a beautiful aroma. In contrast to those of other parts of the world, African mangoes are very large, usually with thick, traffic-light skin: red, green, and golden orange. Traditionally, the coconut milk would be made from fresh coconuts, but you may use canned milk instead if this is not an option for you. Just be sure to check that it is unsweetened!*

INGREDIENTS

1	onion, diced
1 tsp	curry powder
1 tsp	turmeric
2	cloves of garlic, minced
1/4	cabbage, chopped
4–5 cups	stir fry veggies of your choice (bell peppers, carrots, broccoli, etc)
optional	meat substitute (e.g., seitan)
2–3	chilis, chopped finely
2	mangos
1 1/2 cups	vegetable stock
1 cup	coconut milk
	salt and pepper, to taste

DIRECTIONS

1   Heat a large, non-stick saucepan on medium-heat with 2–3 T of a neutral oil. Add the onions, garlic, curry powder, and turmeric and sauté, stirring occasionally, until onions are semi-translucent.

2   Add in the chopped cabbage and sauté for a few minutes. If using a meat substitute, sauté it with the cabbage until lightly browned.

3   Stir in the remaining veggies, chilis, coconut milk, and stock. Cover and simmer for 15 minutes.

4   Cut one of the mangoes into cubes and purée the other. Add both to the curry.

5   Simmer, covered, for 10 minutes.

6   Serve with basmati rice and flatbread.

Galey iyo Qumbo

Corn in coconut-turmeric sauce

Serves 4-6

If the corn has not been ground into flour, it might be simmered in a coconut-curry sauce—warm, rich, and decadent. Yet, the dish remains light and healthy. The corn simmers in a bubbling pot of seasoned, salted coconut milk—spiced, but not spicy. The addition of tomato sauce bespeaks the Italian colonial occupation, which dominated the country from the end of the nineteenth century to the first half of the twentieth century.

Recipes and information on Somali food provided by Abderazzaq Noor and Shukri Abdikarim of The Somali Kitchen (www.somalikitchen.com).

INGREDIENTS

3 ears	corn on the cob, cut into halves or thirds
1	onion
1 can	coconut milk = 13.5 oz
1 cup	water
1/2 cup	puréed tomatoes (not tomato paste)
1 tsp	turmeric
	salt and pepper, to taste

DIRECTIONS

1　Dice the onion finely and set aside.

2　Arrange the corn pieces evenly in a large saucepan and cook on medium heat with onions, coconut milk, water, turmeric, and tomato purée.

3　Bring to boil. Then lower the heat and simmer for around 20 minutes, or until the corn is cooked through. Turn the pieces occasionally so that the flavors of the sauce are infused evenly throughout the corn.

4　Serve next to rice, millet, or bread. The sauce can be ladled over the grain like a curry.

Misir iyo Lows

Nutty lentil salad

Serves 4

INGREDIENTS

2 cups	lentils, boiled
2	tomatoes
1	onion, chopped
1–2	chilies
1 tsp	turmeric
1 tsp	curry powder
1/2 cup	walnut pieces
1/4 cup	slivered almonds
2 T	oil
	salt and pepper, to taste

DIRECTIONS

1   Heat the oil in a pan on medium-high. When hot, add the turmeric and curry powder and fry for a few minutes, stirring, to release the flavors.

2   Slice the chilies finely and add them to the pan along with the walnuts. Cook for a few minutes until lightly toasted.

3   Add the remaining ingredients and sauté until warm all the way through.

4   Serve warm as a side dish or cool as a salad.

Recipes and information on Somali food provided by Abderazzaq Noor and Shukri Abdikarim of The Somali Kitchen (www.somalikitchen.com).

Maraq Baamiye

Okra with tomato and spices

Serves 6

"While much of the Somali diet is meat-based, there are many vegetarian dishes. Somali food is a rich and spicy mix of flavors from the Horn of Africa, East Africa, the Middle East, India, and as far as Italy! Okra is one of my favourite vegetarian dishes. The mix of okra and spices, the sweetness of the tomato and the tanginess of the tamarind or lemon, creates a wonderful explosion of flavor. The addition of lemon or tamarind eliminates the sticky substance that okra releases when cooked. In Somali, we call this wonderful vegetable baamiye Maraq—*okra with sauce. Maraq Baamiye goes well with any kind of flatbread or steamed rice. Leftovers are great as a sandwich filling. This recipe is from our food blog www.somalikitchen.com, which we started because it was a great way to combine our passions—food, cooking, eating, writing and Somali culture."*

Abderazzaq Noor & Shukri Abdikarim
www.somalikitchen.com

INGREDIENTS

500g	fresh or frozen okra, washed and sliced
2	tomatoes, diced
1 T	tomato paste
1	onion, diced
1/2 tsp	mustard seeds
1	clove garlic, minced
2	green chilies, diced, or 1 tsp ground red chili powder (optional)
1 tsp	cumin
1 tsp	coriander powder
1 tsp	turmeric
1 T	tamarid paste or lemon juice
4 T	olive oil
	small bunch of fresh coriander leaves
	handful dried fenugreek leaves
1 tsp	sugar
	salt and pepper, to taste

DIRECTIONS

1   Heat your oil in a pan. When sizzling hot, add the mustard seeds, stirring occasionally with a wooden spoon.

2   As soon as they start to pop, add the remaining ingredients.

3   Cook for 20 minutes, stirring occasionally until the okra is tender and the liquid has almost evaporated. You may add 1/4 cup water if you prefer it soupier.

PALESTINE

فلسطين

Palestinian customs are ancient, dating far back to the agricultural, rural societies that lived on the banks of the River Jordan. Cities such as Hebron, Gaza, Al Quds (Jerusalem), and Nazareth were trading centers whose pace of life contrasted with the seasonal calendars of farming villages. There is therefore great variety in this small stretch of land.

Palestine has witnessed many epochs. Over the years, social customs evolved and adapted to contemporary norms. Urban centers grew, as did the professional classes inhabiting them. When the Palestinians were expelled from their land in 1948 with the creation of Israel—an event known as the *Nakba*, or "catastrophe"—the culture continued to evolve, reflecting the resilient nature of collective identity. In the decades after the Nakba, 90 percent of Palestinians who lived in what is today called Israel were expelled, and 550 villages were completely destroyed. By 1958, 5,000 Palestinians had been shot dead by Israeli border patrols for trying to return to their homes. A decade later, another 120,000 Gazans were expelled with a prohibition on their return. Today, food remains one of the (increasingly few) avenues Palestinians in diaspora still have access to through which they can explore and experience their culture, even in an age of political, legal, and social uncertainty.

Militarization of life

Since the occupation began in 1967, the Israeli military has controlled all Gaza and West Bank borders, and therefore regulated the flow of goods and humans. Palestine does not have its own airport. Consequently, areas that were almost entirely dependent on religious tourism, such as Bethlehem, have experienced severe economic collapse. Roadblocks, checkpoints, and denials of permits contribute to a systematic assault on Palestinian livelihood. The free movement of technology and weapons across international borders, many of which land in the armories of the Israeli military, provide a stark contrast to the physical segregation of Palestinians under Israeli occupation. Some Gazans will never be able to leave the confines of the walled-in city in which they are trapped, which happens to be the most densely populated place on Earth.

Food Security in Occupied Palestine

In 2000, martial restrictions intensified, with Palestinians being at times prevented from entering Israel, unable to move between parts of the occupied territories, or forced to abide by curfew.

- In just two years, per capita GDP fell 40 percent (World Bank 2003).

- 20 percent of households lost all income, while the majority lost at least half (UNSCO, 4).

- Unemployment rose from 10 to 40 percent, with some areas rising to 70 percent unemployment (World Bank 2004A, I).

- Poverty rose from 25 to 60 percent between 2000 and 2003 (World Bank 2003).

- Food consumption declined by 25 percent (World Bank 2004, 36).

- More than 40 percent of Gazans were "entirely dependent" on food aid during this period (Bennet).

- Malnutrition rates maintained a relatively low level until a major spike in 2002. Within a year, 13 percent of children were considered acutely malnourished (World Bank 2004, 37).

GAZA WATER CONFINED & CONTAMINATED

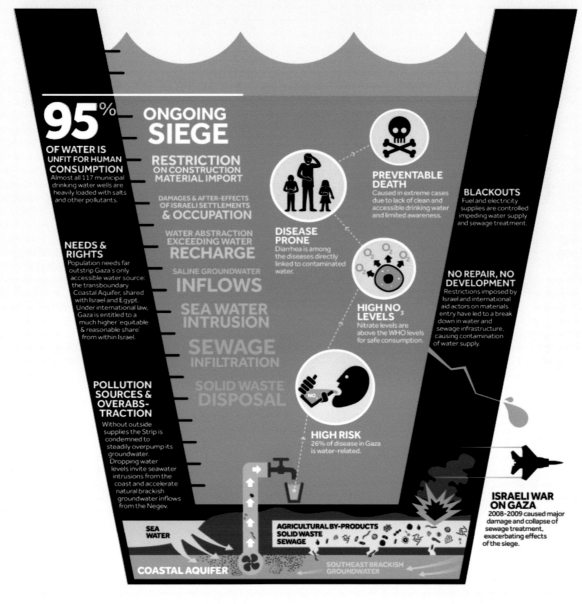

95% OF WATER IS UNFIT FOR HUMAN CONSUMPTION
Almost all 117 municipal drinking water wells are heavily loaded with salts and other pollutants.

NEEDS & RIGHTS
Population needs far outstrip Gaza's only accessible water source: the transboundary Coastal Aquifer, shared with Israel and Egypt. Under international law, Gaza is entitled to a much higher 'equitable & reasonable share' from within Israel.

POLLUTION SOURCES & OVERABSTRACTION
Without outside supplies the Strip is condemned to steadily overpump its groundwater. Dropping water levels invite seawater intrusions from the coast and accelerate natural brackish groundwater inflows from the Negev.

ONGOING SIEGE

RESTRICTION ON CONSTRUCTION MATERIAL IMPORT

DAMAGES & AFTER-EFFECTS OF ISRAELI SETTLEMENTS & OCCUPATION

WATER ABSTRACTION EXCEEDING WATER RECHARGE

SALINE GROUNDWATER INFLOWS

SEA WATER INTRUSION

SEWAGE INFILTRATION

SOLID WASTE DISPOSAL

DISEASE PRONE
Diarrhea is among the diseases directly linked to contaminated water.

PREVENTABLE DEATH
Caused in extreme cases due to lack of clean and accessible drinking water and limited awareness.

HIGH NO$_3$ LEVELS
Nitrate levels are above the WHO levels for safe consumption.

HIGH RISK
26% of disease in Gaza is water-related.

BLACKOUTS
Fuel and electricity supplies are controlled impeding water supply and sewage treatment.

NO REPAIR, NO DEVELOPMENT
Restrictions imposed by Israel and international aid actors on materials entry have led to a break down in water and sewage infrastructure, causing contamination of water supply.

ISRAELI WAR ON GAZA
2008-2009 caused major damage and collapse of sewage treatment, exacerbating effects of the siege.

SEA WATER

AGRICULTURAL BY-PRODUCTS SOLID WASTE SEWAGE

COASTAL AQUIFER

SOUTHEAST BRACKISH GROUNDWATER

SOURCES
B'tselem, 2000, Thirsty for a Solution: The Water Shortage in the Occupied Territories and its Solution in the Final Status Agreement, p 59.
C. Messerschmid, Birzeit University, 2011, Water in Gaza: Problems and Prospects, p 3, 6, 20-21.
Blue Planet and LifeSource, 2012, The Human Right to Water in Palestine: In Our Right to Water, pp 4-5.
OCHA, August 2009, Locked In: The Humanitarian Impact of Two Years of Blockade of the Gaza Strip, pp 4, 22, 23.
Save the Children and Medical Aid for Palestine, 2012, Gaza's Children: Falling Behind. The effect of the blockade on child health in Gaza, pp 5, 16, 17.
Thirsting for Justice, 2003, Right to Water in oPT, pp 19, 29.
UNICEF, March 2011, Protecting Children from Unsafe Water in Gaza, pp 7, 9, 10, 16.
World Bank, 2009, Assessment of Restrictions on Palestinian Water Sector Development - West Bank and Gaza - pp 27, 29, 30 (Original source: Fieldwork interviews: WHO, Gaza city, November 24).

REVISION 01
29 AUG 2012

VISUALIZING**PALESTINE**

WWW.VISUALIZINGPALESTINE.ORG, AUGUST 2012
SHARE AND DISTRIBUTE FREELY. CREATIVE COMMONS BY-NC-ND 3.0 LICENSE.

@visualizingpal
fb.com/visualizingpalestine

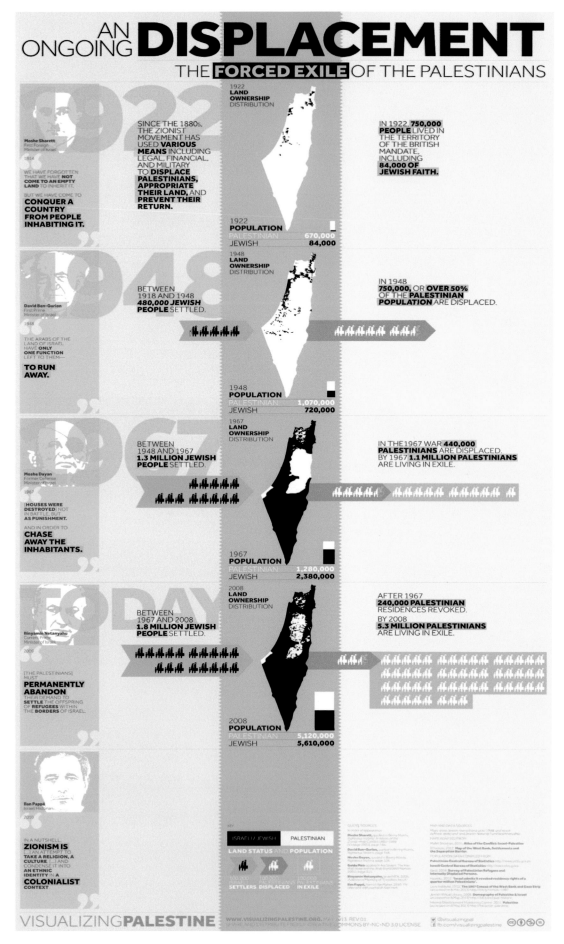

AN ONGOING DISPLACEMENT

THE FORCED EXILE OF THE PALESTINIANS

1922

Moshe Sharett
First Foreign
Minister of Israel
1914

WE HAVE FORGOTTEN THAT WE HAVE **NOT COME TO AN EMPTY LAND** TO INHERIT IT.

BUT WE HAVE COME TO **CONQUER A COUNTRY FROM PEOPLE INHABITING IT.**

SINCE THE 1880s, THE ZIONIST MOVEMENT HAS USED **VARIOUS MEANS** INCLUDING LEGAL, FINANCIAL, AND MILITARY TO **DISPLACE PALESTINIANS, APPROPRIATE THEIR LAND,** AND **PREVENT THEIR RETURN.**

1922 **LAND OWNERSHIP** DISTRIBUTION

IN 1922, **750,000 PEOPLE** LIVED IN THE TERRITORY OF THE BRITISH MANDATE, INCLUDING **84,000 OF JEWISH FAITH.**

1922 **POPULATION**
PALESTINIAN 670,000
JEWISH 84,000

1948

David Ben-Gurion
First Prime
Minister of Israel
1948

THE ARABS OF THE LAND OF ISRAEL HAVE **ONLY ONE FUNCTION** LEFT TO THEM— **TO RUN AWAY.**

BETWEEN 1918 AND 1948 **480,000 JEWISH PEOPLE** SETTLED.

1948 **LAND OWNERSHIP** DISTRIBUTION

IN 1948 **750,000, OR OVER 50%** OF THE **PALESTINIAN POPULATION** ARE DISPLACED.

1948 **POPULATION**
PALESTINIAN 1,070,000
JEWISH 720,000

1967

Moshe Dayan
Former Defense
Minister of Israel
1967

[HOUSES WERE **DESTROYED**] NOT IN BATTLE, BUT **AS PUNISHMENT.**

AND IN ORDER TO **CHASE AWAY THE INHABITANTS.**

BETWEEN 1948 AND 1967 **1.3 MILLION JEWISH PEOPLE** SETTLED.

1967 **LAND OWNERSHIP** DISTRIBUTION

IN THE 1967 WAR **440,000 PALESTINIANS** ARE DISPLACED. BY 1967 **1.1 MILLION PALESTINIANS** ARE LIVING IN EXILE.

1967 **POPULATION**
PALESTINIAN 1,280,000
JEWISH 2,380,000

TODAY

Binyamin Netanyahu
Current Prime
Minister of Israel
2008

[THE PALESTINIANS] MUST **PERMANENTLY ABANDON** THEIR DEMAND TO **SETTLE** THE OFFSPRING OF **REFUGEES** WITHIN THE **BORDERS** OF ISRAEL.

BETWEEN 1967 AND 2008 **1.8 MILLION JEWISH PEOPLE** SETTLED.

2008 **LAND OWNERSHIP** DISTRIBUTION

AFTER 1967 **240,000 PALESTINIAN** RESIDENCES REVOKED. BY 2008 **5.3 MILLION PALESTINIANS** ARE LIVING IN EXILE.

2008 **POPULATION**
PALESTINIAN 5,120,000
JEWISH 5,610,000

Ilan Pappé
Israeli Historian
2010

IN A NUTSHELL, **ZIONISM IS** [...] AN ATTEMPT TO TAKE A RELIGION, A CULTURE [...] AND CONDENSE IT INTO AN ETHNIC IDENTITY IN A **COLONIALIST** CONTEXT

KEY

ISRAELI / JEWISH   PALESTINIAN

LAND STATUS AND **POPULATION**

SETTLERS   DISPLACED   IN EXILE

VISUALIZING**PALESTINE**

WWW.VISUALIZINGPALESTINE.ORG, MAY 2013, REV.01.

@visualizingpal
fb.com/visualizingpalestine

250

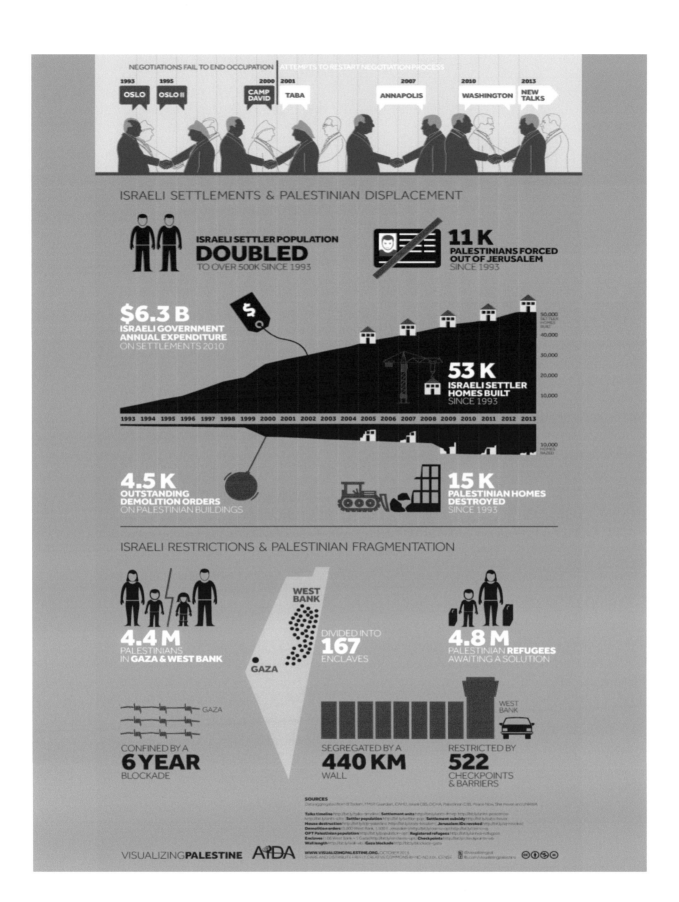

Spaciocide

"Spaciocide" refers to the dispossession, occupation, and destruction of Palestinian living space. This tactic is exercised with the intention of emptying the land of Palestinian people, to be subsequently seized by the Israeli state. Historical Palestine was advertised as a "land without people for a people without a land." This claim makes explicit the Zionist figuring of the 800,000 Palestinians who were on the land, and were expelled from it, as non-persons. Between 1948 and 1965, the entire region where Arabs resided was made into a "military zone." The Occupied Palestinian Territories (OPTs) remained so from 1967 until Oslo (Hanafi). The categorization of Palestinians into discrete identities intensifies the militarization of daily life, and attempts to preclude the unification of the Palestinians into a single nation. The Palestinian state is weakened in every sense, from its division into disconnected enclaves, each surrounded by walls, settlement blocs, and military closures. Israeli Military Order 101 prohibits all gatherings of ten or more people "for a political purpose or for a matter that could be interpreted as political" without the permission of the Israeli military commander in the area (Amnesty).

Palestinians are divided ontologically—as refugees, citizens, stateless people, residents—but also geographically: the OPTs are divided into zones A, B, B-, B+, C, H1, and H. Each zone represents a different distribution of power between the Palestinian Authority and the Israeli military. Area C takes up 61 percent of the West Bank but is directly under Israeli administration. The Israeli state refuses to grant building permits to Palestinians there, and the PA has no authority to intervene.

The militarized division of land affects every aspect of Palestinian life. The wall reinforces the disciplinary power of the state and constructs the OPTs as open-air prisons, thus implicating those who live within them as dangerous criminals.

Hospitals in Gaza suffer, like the rest of the city, from very limited access to electricity, but also from a blockade, which restricts their ability to access medicines, equipment, and personnel. Those hoping to seek treatment, even in the Palestinian West Bank (let alone Israel), can seldom do so. People can spend days at checkpoints, where they routinely suffer humiliation and contempt at the hands of young Israeli soldiers, fresh out of high school. If they are able to access treatment in Israel, sick Palestinians may not have time for anything else but to merely survive, since such access would necessitate long bus rides through cities followed by long walks through towns, long waits at checkpoints, and long drives to the hospital, only to have to repeat it all a couple of hours later. It is not only land that is stolen, but also time.

In addition to checkpoints, the state maintains separate roads for Israelis and Palestinians in the OPTs. Soldiers monitor roadblocks and fences, which not only restrict Palestinian movement, but amount to a fortification that authorizes and aggravates Israeli fears about Palestinians. According to B'Tselem, the Israeli Information Center for Human Rights in the Occupied Territories, there are an estimated 622,670 settlers in the West Bank. In Hebron, 200,000 Palestinians are prohibited from entering the old city center, which had formed part of the fabric of life for centuries, but is now home to fewer than a thousand Jewish settlers, protected by a thousand Israeli soldiers.

The strict regulatory constrictions placed upon Palestinians have weakened their ability to effectively coordinate on-the-ground resistance. Furthermore, in the context of Israeli occupation, control of movement is a formidable demonstration of biopower, establishing the state as the ultimate arbiter of life and death in Palestine. It is perhaps for this reason that online transnational solidarity has been met with such enthusiasm.

The construction of the "apartheid wall," which reaches up to eight feet in some places, does not cut across the land in a straight line, and nor does it follow natural boundaries. Rather, it cuts through villages, around fields and blocked archaeological sites. The Israeli state justifies the construction of the (illegal) wall as a measure to protect Israelis from Palestinian terrorist attacks—but if that were the case, a simple division along the green line would have sufficed. The peculiar route the wall takes points to a different motive: the wall was a land grab, which expropriated more territory for settlers and deprived Palestinian towns of two primary sources of making a living—tourism and agriculture.

The wall cuts through biblical sites in Bethlehem, blocking centuries-old pilgrimage routes and making it extremely difficult for tourists to visit. Even if they can get access, the intense militarization of the checkpoints is hardly inviting.

Community

Family life is a major aspect of Palestinian culture. The political and social climate Palestinians are subjected to has strengthened these values. In the absence of state support, a free economy, or almost any political autonomy, Palestinians have increasingly turned to informal social and organizational networks to fill the gaps of these institutions. Students turn to neighbors, community groups, and extended families when seeking funding for education. Extended families may choose to reside near one another, since Palestinian children are raised to respect their elders and will often support their parents and grandparents when they grow older. Elder relatives, in turn, may play active roles in the care and education of the younger members. The need to retain physical closeness is compounded by the memories of forced separation. Palestinians have, at various times, been severed from family members by Israeli checkpoints, walls, and legal barriers that contained them or their family members, or restricted their ability to move.

Palestinian culture is based on hospitality. This sense of welcoming is extended not only to family members and neighbors, but also passersby.

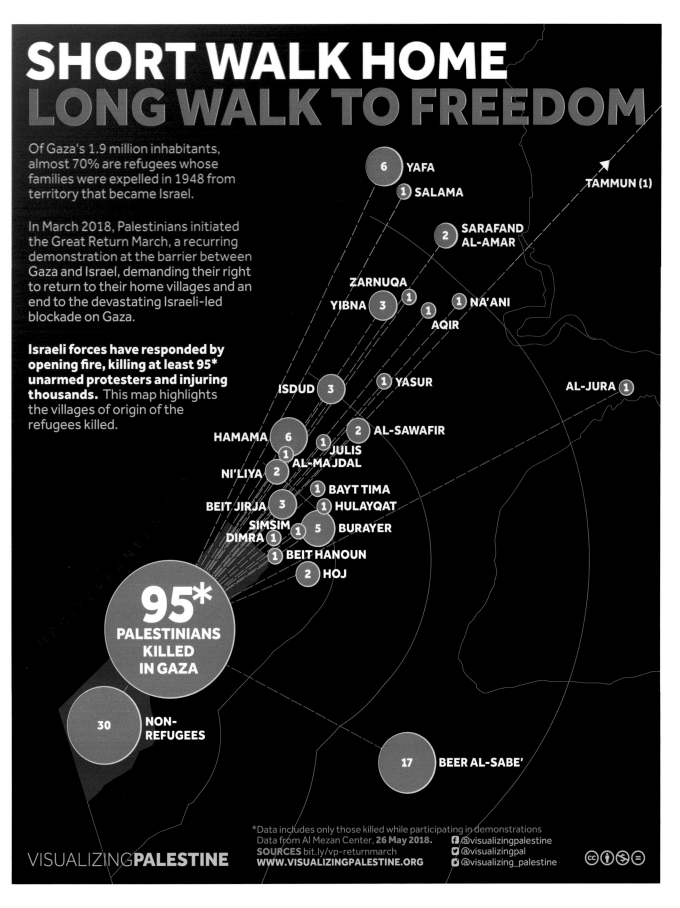

SHORT WALK HOME
LONG WALK TO FREEDOM

Of Gaza's 1.9 million inhabitants, almost 70% are refugees whose families were expelled in 1948 from territory that became Israel.

In March 2018, Palestinians initiated the Great Return March, a recurring demonstration at the barrier between Gaza and Israel, demanding their right to return to their home villages and an end to the devastating Israeli-led blockade on Gaza.

Israeli forces have responded by opening fire, killing at least 95* unarmed protesters and injuring thousands. This map highlights the villages of origin of the refugees killed.

6 YAFA
1 SALAMA
TAMMUN (1)
2 SARAFAND AL-AMAR
ZARNUQA
1
YIBNA 3
1 NA'ANI
1 AQIR
1 YASUR
ISDUD 3
AL-JURA 1
HAMAMA 6
2 AL-SAWAFIR
1 JULIS
1 AL-MAJDAL
NI'LIYA 2
BEIT JIRJA 3
1 BAYT TIMA
1 HULAYQAT
SIMSIM 1
5 BURAYER
DIMRA 1
1 BEIT HANOUN
2 HOJ

95*
PALESTINIANS KILLED IN GAZA

30 NON-REFUGEES

17 BEER AL-SABE'

*Data includes only those killed while participating in demonstrations
*Data from Al Mezan Center, **26 May 2018.***
SOURCES bit.ly/vp-returnmarch
WWW.VISUALIZINGPALESTINE.ORG

🅵 @visualizingpalestine
🐦 @visualizingpal
📷 @visualizing_palestine

VISUALIZING**PALESTINE**

WE
CANT LIVE
SO WE ARE WAITING FOR DEATH
2010 AïDA
CAMP
BETHLEHEM
TAHIA FALISTIN

Israeli Wall, Palestinian Painting. Photo: GEFHunter, iStock

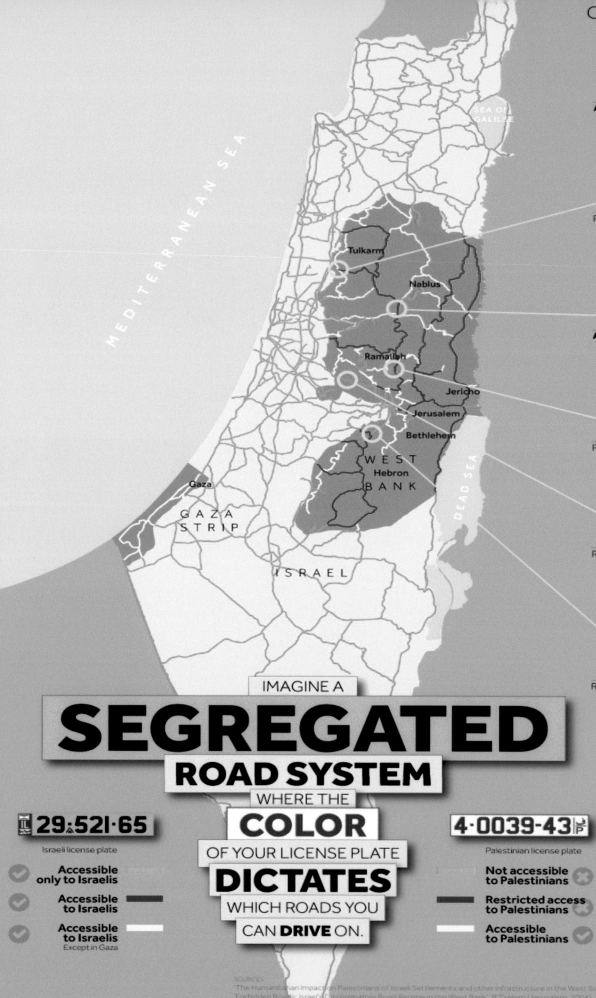

MEDITERRANEAN SEA

SEA OF GALILEE

Tulkarm

Nablus

Ramallah

Jericho

Jerusalem

Bethlehem

W E S T

Hebron

B A N K

DEAD SEA

Gaza

G A Z A
S T R I P

I S R A E L

1   **ALL** RDS   Land expropriated by Israel on either side of major roads.

100 - 150 m

2   ROAD **557**   Underpass roads between Palestinian enclaves, with access often restricted by ga...

3   **ALL** RDS   Checkpoints along and adjacent to all restricted roads.

4   ROAD **45**   Fully segregated road running in parallel to one another.

5   ROAD **443**   Road blocks/trenches prevent access to ma... roads and travel betw... Palestinian enclaves.

6   ROAD **60**   Israeli-only bridges an... tunnels connecting Isr... settlements east of th... separation wall.

IMAGINE A

SEGREGATED

ROAD SYSTEM

WHERE THE

COLOR

OF YOUR LICENSE PLATE

DICTATES

WHICH ROADS YOU

CAN **DRIVE** ON.

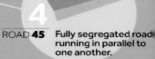
29·52I·65
Israeli license plate

- ✓ **Accessible only to Israelis**
- ✓ **Accessible to Israelis**
- ✓ **Accessible to Israelis** Except in Gaza

4·0039-43
Palestinian license plate

- ✗ **Not accessible to Palestinians**
- ✗ **Restricted access to Palestinians**
- ✓ **Accessible to Palestinians**

ROADS IN THE **WEST BANK**

Israeli-only **79** km

Restricted ...

SOURCES
'The Humanitarian Impact on Palestinians of Israeli Settlements and other Infrastructure in the West Bank', UN OCHA (Jerusalem, 2007)
'Forbidden Roads: Israel's Discriminatory Road Regime in the West Bank', B'Tselem (Jerusalem, 2004)
'Apartheid Roads: Promoting Settlements, Punishing Palestinians', Ma'an Development Center (Ramallah/Gaza, 2008)
openstreetmap.org

VISUALIZINGPALESTINE

UPROOTED.

SINCE 1967 ISRAELI AUTHORITIES HAVE UPROOTED 800,000 PALESTINIAN OLIVE TREES, EQUAL TO 33 CENTRAL PARKS.

800,000 TREES UPROOTED

33x CENTRAL PARK

$ 12.3 MILLION LOST INCOME EACH YEAR TO 80,000 PALESTINIAN FAMILIES WHO RELY ECONOMICALLY ON THE OLIVE HARVEST.

$12.3M ANNUAL LOSS

80,000 FAMILIES AFFECTED

SOURCES | **800,000 olive trees uprooted.** Oxfam, 2011. Olive Harvest Factsheet, p2 | **24,000 trees in Central Park.** Central Park, 2013. Official Website, Frequently Asked Questions (accessed 31 May 2013) | **$12.3 million loss** = 10% of potential peak year income

The combination of racism and capitalism within the state renders the Palestinian body an object of utility for the state to profit off. The appropriation of national symbols and the transformation of hummus and falafel from Levantine specialities into the "national food of Israel" is not only equivalent to rubbing salt (and sumac) into the wound, but to selling the very life and blood flowing out of it.

Falafel / فلافل

Falafel is one of the most famous Arab culinary exports in the world. Although you can find it almost anywhere, falafel originated in what was known as "greater Syria," which was comprised of Jordan, Lebanon, Palestine, and modern-day Syria. In Egypt, falafel is sometimes made with fava beans, and this version is called *ta'miyya*. In Yemen, a variation exists using black-eyed peas, called *bajiyya*.

In all its varieties, falafel is an immensely popular food across the Middle East and North Africa. It is used as a meat replacement for Christians fasting in Lent. In fact, origins of the Egyptian fava-bean version are attributed to the ancient Egyptian Copts, one of the world's oldest Christian communities, dating back to 42 CE.

The earliest records of falafel are from medieval cookbooks of the tenth, thirteenth, and fourteenth centuries. These vegetarian dishes were collectively called *muzawwarat*, referring to their resemblance to meat and efficacy as a substitute. It was generally held among these medieval physicians that these foods were to be given to the poor and sick since they contributed to greater health and digestion than animal proteins.

Falafel was introduced into the Iraqi mainstream largely by the Palestinians who were expelled from their homes in the 1948 *Nakba*. Like elsewhere in the region, it grew in popularity to one of the most ubiquitous forms of street food available. However, in Iraq, the falafel is usually served in Sammoun bread, instead of pita.

One can play around with different combos, adding the delicious morsels into salads, rice dishes, sandwiches, or even fashioning them into burger patties. The perfect falafel is crispy on the outside but tender on the inside. It should melt in your mouth. For a lighter version, try baking them instead.

INGREDIENTS

2 cups	chickpeas: dried, soaked overnight, and rinsed
1	large onion, diced
4	cloves of garlic, minced
1 bunch	parsley
1 bunch	coriander
1 tsp	salt
1/2 tsp	chili flakes, dried
1 tsp	cumin
2 tsp	baking soda
3 T	flour
	olive oil

NOTE: using canned chickpeas will result in a completely different texture and could cause the patty to fall apart.

DIRECTIONS

1   Pulse the chickpeas in a food processor until they resemble a coarse breadcrumb. Set aside.

2   Blend the remaining ingredients minus the baking powder into a paste. Using your hands, mix the paste into the ground chickpeas. If it feels too dry and crumbly, add water, a few drops at a time, until the consistency improves.

3   Pour olive oil up to 1-inch deep in a frying pan and turn the heat to medium. While the oil is heating up, sprinkle the baking soda over the falafel mix. Knead and roll into golf-ball sized balls. This makes about 25 falafels.

4   Drop one falafel into the pan. If the oil is hot enough, it will sizzle immediately. After 2–3 minutes, the falafel should be golden brown in color and able to retain its shape. Transfer onto a plate lined with paper towels to absorb the excess oil. Repeat with the remaining mixture.

5   Sprinkle with coarse salt while still hot and drizzle with lemony-tahini sauce (p. 75).

Religion in Palestine

Christians and Muslims have lived alongside one another in Palestine for centuries, which lends a harmony to the entire area of Palestine. This harmony imbues Palestine with a special beauty. A perfect representation of this spiritual harmony can be found in Manger Square, Bethlehem, where the Church of the Nativity and the Mosque of Omar bin al-Khattab share a space.

Easter in Palestine is also an occasion for celebration with family. Observances begin with Palm Sunday, when families in Jerusalem's Christian Quarter prepare palm branches decorated with flowers and ribbons for the annual procession from Bethphage, a village on the eastern slopes of the Mount of Olives, to the Church of St. Anne inside Jerusalem's Old City. At the procession's end, Christian and Muslim Boy Scouts from all parts of Palestine circle the Old City walls, waving flags and playing music. Palestinian families celebrate Christmas with gift-giving, carols, and traditional meals of roast lamb, sweets made with nougat and sesame seeds, roasted chestnuts, a hot, sweet drink of rosewater, and semolina pancakes stuffed with nuts and cheese.

On Good Friday, Palestinian Christians and pilgrims from around the world mark the Stations of the Cross, along the Via Dolorosa. Easter observances culminate with *Sabt an-Nur*, or Saturday of Light, which commemorates the resurrection of Christ. Hundreds of pilgrims sleep overnight by the Church of the Holy Sepulchre, waiting to receive the "light" from the Greek Orthodox Patriarch, who leads a procession to the site of Jesus' tomb. After prayer and meditation, the flame from Jesus' tomb is used to light candles carried by the faithful from village to village, and town to town. Crowds of people gather in village, town, and city centers to welcome the flame and greet each other by saying, *al-Massih Qam*, or "Christ is risen." In the largely Christian city of Ramallah, Boy Scouts parade in the streets in full uniform, with drums, banners, and flags, and march towards the Greek Orthodox church where the Easter service takes place.

For Muslims, Eid al-Fitr, the Fast-Breaking Feast, marks the end of the month of Ramadan, believed to be the month in which the Prophet Muhammad began receiving his divine revelation. Throughout the month, from sunrise to sunset, Muslims abstain from food and drink. Families and friends gather each evening at sunset to break their fast together. The fast is traditionally broken with dates and juice or milk, followed by light meals and sweets, like *qatayef*, a sweet, stuffed pancake. In Palestine, men often congregate at the mosque each evening for *taraweeh* prayers. One section of the Quran is read each evening, the result being that the entire holy book has been read by the end of the month. Eid al-Fitr is a joyous occasion that brings families together. The entire atmosphere is one of sharing—food, gratitude, and company. Ramadan is also a time of almsgiving for Muslims in Palestine and all over the Muslim world, with money and food given in large amounts to the less fortunate.

Left: Dome of the Rock. Photo: bgcurtis, Pixabay

pp. 266–267: Church of the Nativity. Photo: David Rodrigo, Unsplash

pp. 270–271: Al Aqsa Mosque. Photo: John T @john_visualz, Unsplash

Christmas festivities in Bethlehem begin with prayers and songs nine days before Christmas Day. On Christmas Eve, the Patriarch of Jerusalem makes a traditional procession through Bethlehem and the faithful gather in Manger Square and the Church of the Nativity at midnight to celebrate the birth of Jesus. For centuries, they have been joined by pilgrims from around the world. Traditionally coming in the hundreds, the numbers of pilgrims have dwindled to the tens of thousands in recent years.

Tea

Black tea is a staple in most Middle Eastern cultures, with Palestine being no exception.

Tea is served with sugar or honey in transparent glasses so the drinker may judge the potency of the brew. Sometimes other herbs are added for additional flavors or medicinal qualities.

Aside from black tea, Palestinians enjoy many herbal blends, including *maramiya* (sage), *baboonej* (chamomile), *n'na'* (mint), and *shih* (wormwood).

Beyond sustenance, drinking tea is a social activity in Palestinian culture. It is to be shared, perhaps with a *ma'moul* cookie or some fresh dates on the side. A guest in a Palestinian home will never want for warmth, kindness, or food. The doors are always open—and the water perpetually boiled—for guests.

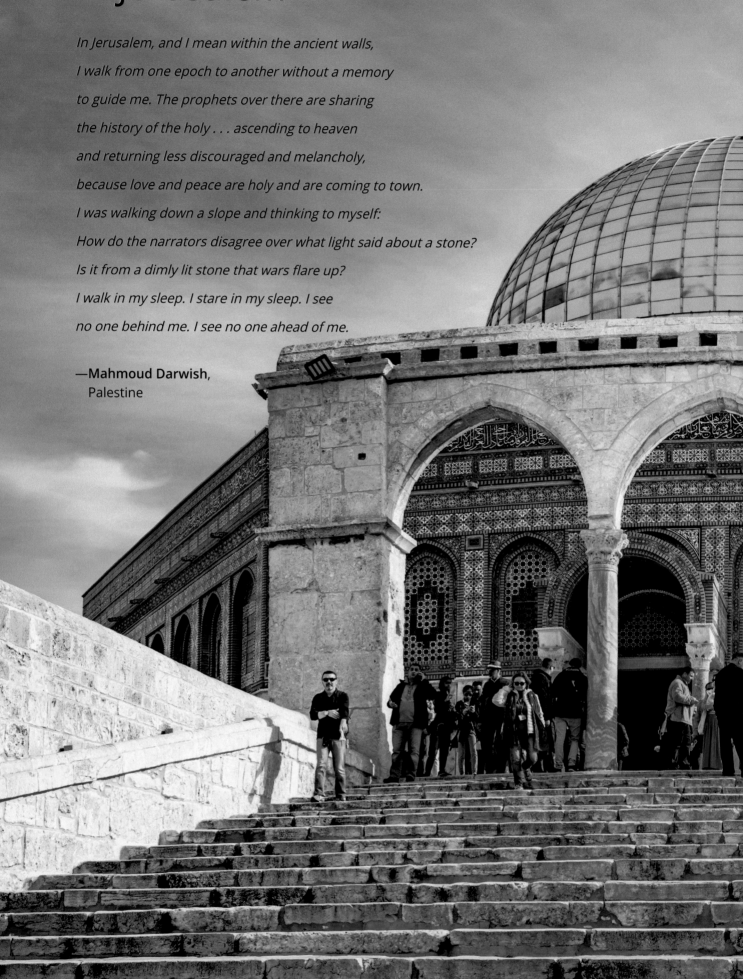

In Jerusalem

In Jerusalem, and I mean within the ancient walls,

I walk from one epoch to another without a memory

to guide me. The prophets over there are sharing

the history of the holy . . . ascending to heaven

and returning less discouraged and melancholy,

because love and peace are holy and are coming to town.

I was walking down a slope and thinking to myself:

How do the narrators disagree over what light said about a stone?

Is it from a dimly lit stone that wars flare up?

I walk in my sleep. I stare in my sleep. I see

no one behind me. I see no one ahead of me.

—**Mahmoud Darwish,**
  Palestine

GRAINS

Bulgur Salad with Date-Glazed Roasted Carrots 279

Rice with Mushrooms and Truffle 281

Filo Pastry *Pulau/Polow* 285
  Filo pastry rice cake

Mujadarra 289
  Rice with lentils and caramelized onions

Lubia Polow 301
  Persian tomato and green-bean rice

Dolmeh Felfel 305
  Peppers stuffed with rice

The Fertile Crescent

The "Cradle of Civilization"

More than fifty archaeological excavations conducted over the past half-century have determined the Fertile Crescent to be the home of the first agricultural farmers, and also the first spot where sheep, cattle, and goats were domesticated. The Fertile Crescent is a region of the Middle East out of which some of the earliest human civilizations emerged. For this reason, it is also known as the "Cradle of Civilization." It was also the birthplace of a number of technological innovations, including the wheel, written language, and the use of irrigation and aqueducts. In addition, almost every intellectual field was advanced during this period, from mathematics and astronomy to medicine, science, and cosmology. The Crescent's western point begins at the Nile River on the Sinai Peninsula, from which it traverses Palestine, Lebanon, and Syria (all of which used to be known as "greater Syria"), extends over the Mesopotamian plains, through present-day Iraq. It also crosses into parts of present-day Egypt, Jordan, Turkey, Israel, Saudi Arabia, Iran, and Kuwait. Its arteries are the Tigris and Euphrates rivers, which flow through the heart of the once-abundant region.

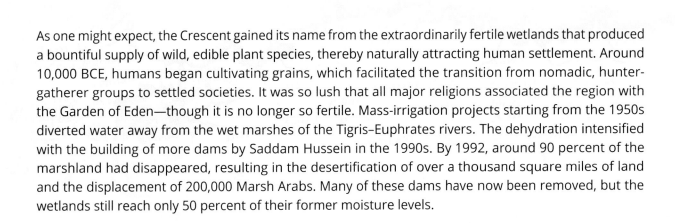

As one might expect, the Crescent gained its name from the extraordinarily fertile wetlands that produced a bountiful supply of wild, edible plant species, thereby naturally attracting human settlement. Around 10,000 BCE, humans began cultivating grains, which facilitated the transition from nomadic, hunter-gatherer groups to settled societies. It was so lush that all major religions associated the region with the Garden of Eden—though it is no longer so fertile. Mass-irrigation projects starting from the 1950s diverted water away from the wet marshes of the Tigris–Euphrates rivers. The dehydration intensified with the building of more dams by Saddam Hussein in the 1990s. By 1992, around 90 percent of the marshland had disappeared, resulting in the desertification of over a thousand square miles of land and the displacement of 200,000 Marsh Arabs. Many of these dams have now been removed, but the wetlands still reach only 50 percent of their former moisture levels.

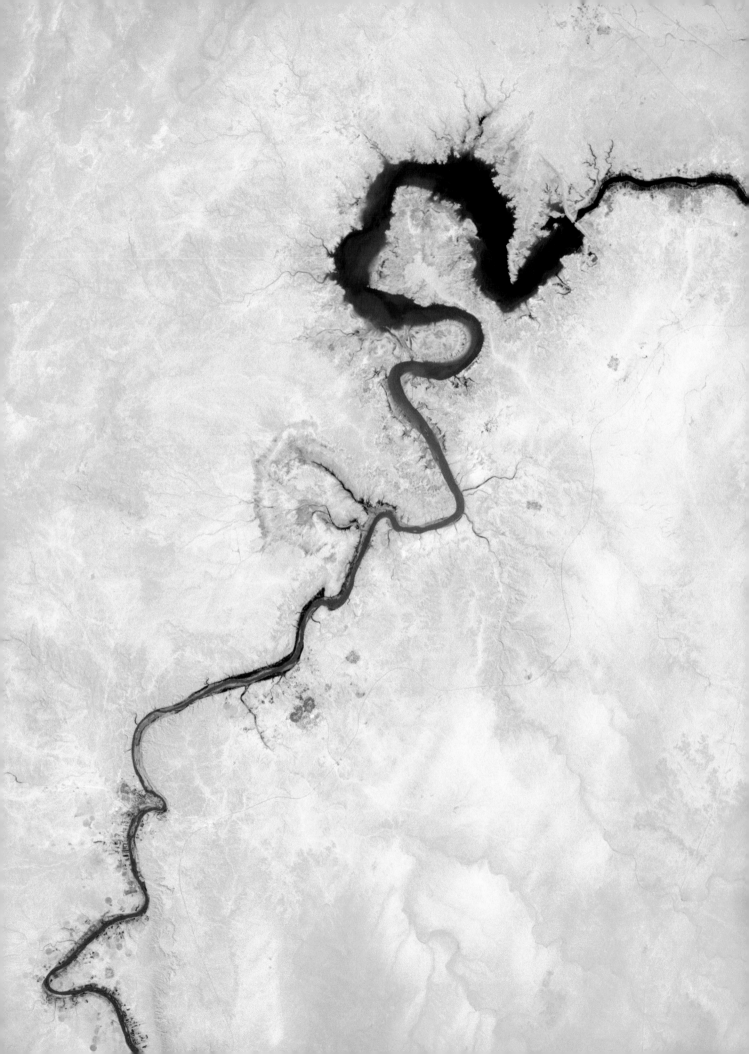

Mesopotamia

Land Between the Rivers

Mesopotamia, in present-day Iraq and Turkey, was home to some of the earliest-known human civilizations. It takes its name from the Greek words, *mesos* (middle) and *potamos* (river). Its Inhabitants lived in round mud-and-brick dwellings alongside the banks of the Tigris and Euphrates. Animals, and then edible plants, such as flax, wheat, pulses, and barley, were domesticted between 11000 and 9000 BCE. Flatbreads were made from barley, while beer was made from wheat—under the patronage of Ninkasi, the Goddess of Beer. The oldest evidence of beer-brewing comes from a Sumerian settlement in present-day Iran. In addition to food, crops were applied to a number of uses. Flax was used to make linen, and date palms were used for crafts. Mesopotamian societies were thus the first to build what might be called "cities."[1] They possessed temples, artisinal production (e.g. pottery), and early-stage formal institutions, including systems of credit, ownership, and the first legal codes .

As Nawal Nasrallah notes in his book, *Delights from the Garden of Eden,* "The first documented recipes in human history were inscribed on the ancient land of Mesopotamia. In the 1930s, three clay tablets written in cuneiform were excavated from the site of ancient Babylon, south of Baghdad. They were deciphered from the Akkadian to modern languages in the 1980s by the French Assyriologist Jean Bottéro. One of them was unfortunately badly damaged, but the other two are in good shape enough to reveal a sophisticated cuisine in the second millennium BCE. Yale University is now the proud host of these precious documents."

The earliest of these cities were built by the Sumerians, who called themselves the *sag-giga*, or the "black-headed ones." They were pioneers in many things. For one, they invented one of the earliest forms of writing, called the cuneiform script. This inaugurated a millennia-long tradition of literature-making and artistic production. The most reknowned of the repository might be the *Epic of Gilgamesh*, a 3,000-line epic poem that follows the life and battles of a Sumer King in a quest for the secret(s) of eternal life. In addition, the Sumerians were among the first humans to use bronze, from which they made a great many things, both funcitonal and ornamental. Their towns were organized with canals for irrigation, and included monuments such as stepped pyramids, called ziggurats. By 4000 BCE, the Sumerians were estimated to have already established around a dozen city-states around present-day Iraq.

The cultivation of grain is said to be one of the most important factors in the development of civilization because it allowed settler societies, such as those in Mesapotamia and Babylonia, to develop trade and other social institutions. Harvest required social organization of workforce, while trade required the construction of routes and caravans, which in turn necessitated institutions that could reduce uncertainty (e.g., forms of protection or allegiance). All of these amalgamated to result in ever-more economic complexity. The relation between grain and trade was not only indirect. In Babylonia and Assyria, barley was widely used as a currency. Similarly, beer was considered a divine gift, a source of nutrition, an intoxicant, and a form of payment across the Crescent.

---

1   *The terminology of "cities" is grounded in modern epistemologies and entails a particular ordering of life that doesn't apply here.*

Bulgur Salad with Date-Glazed Roasted Carrots

Serves 6

This is an Iraqi-inspired salad, using ingredients such as bulgur, dates, and certain spices, which have been in use in the land for millennia. It was here, in the Fertile Crescent, where ancient societies started creating the grain products we know and love from the ancestors of contemporary durum wheat.

INGREDIENTS

5	carrots
2 1/2 cups	chickpeas, cooked
1 cup	dry bulgur
1 bunch	coriander
5 large	medjool dates, chopped
	Arabic spice mix (*baharat*)
ADD-INS	Raisins, pomegranate seeds, flaked almonds, chopped mint
1 bunch	coriander

DRESSING

2 T	date syrup
2 T	olive oil
1/2	lemon, juiced
1	clove of garlic, minced
5 large	medjool dates, chopped

DIRECTIONS

1. Cook bulgur according to instructions on the packet. Take care not to overcook it as you want the grains to be slightly chewy. Allow to cool.

2. Preheat your oven to 400F.

3. In a pan, fry the onion and spices in some olive oil until tender and slightly caramelized.

4. Slice the carrots in half length wise (and again into quarters, if your carrots are particularly large).

5. Assemble them in a lined or non-stick dish with a drizzle of oil and half of the dressing. Bake for 16 minutes until soft.

6. Add the chickpeas to the dish. Mix everything and return to oven for 12 minutes. When cooked, add the bulgur and onion to the dish and toss with the dressing until evenly coated.

7. Top with nuts, pomegranate, herbs, and dried fruit.

Chima (Truffle)

Traditionally, the exotic truffle *chima* is used in cooking this variety of rice, but mushroom is substituted nowadays because it is more readily available, and much cheaper.

The truffle season is very short in Iraq. Truffles appear only during springtime: the season of showers, thunder, and lightning. It was believed that such weather conditions played a role in the formation of these delicacies. They actually play an indirect role. When it thunders, it rains, and when it rains in the desert, the force of the falling water reveals the truffles buried in the sand. They are then picked up by the Bedouins and sold in the markets of the big cities. (**Nasrallah**).

Rice with Mushrooms and Truffle

Serves 4

This dish is usually made with cubed lamb, or can be made vegetarian by leaving out the meat or using a plant-based substitute, such as seitan. In addition, desert truffles are quite different from European truffles, and can be used as a main ingredient due to their being less potent than their European counterparts. They are still expensive, but it would not be unheard of to steam them, salt them, and eat them whole. If you do not have access to whole truffles, simply replace them with white mushrooms and cook using truffle oil.

"Instead of the usual rice and stew, rice is sometimes cooked and simmered with a variety of meats and vegetables in one pot, collectively called *Timman Tacheena*. It is a very convenient dish, usually served with yogurt and salad, an ideal meal for hot summer days." (**Nasrallah**)

INGREDIENTS

2 T	oil
1	medium onion, chopped
450g	desert truffles or whole, white mushrooms (cut into thick chunks if large)
1 tsp	curry powder
1 tsp	noomi basra (crushed dried lime)
1/2 tsp	turmeric
1 tsp	*baharat* (Arabic spice mix)
1 tsp	salt
1/2 tsp	black pepper
1/2 cup	chopped parsely
1 cup	plain white rice

DIRECTIONS

1   In a medium skillet, heat oil and sauté mushrooms, stirring frequently until all moisture evaporates and mushrooms start to brown, for about 15 minutes.

2   Add onion and stir until transparent, for about 5 minutes. In the last 2 minutes of cooking, stir in mushroom, curry powder, noomi Basra, turmeric, salt, pepper, baharat, and parsley. The mixture will emit a wonderful aroma.

3   Cook white rice and immediately empty it into a bowl. Then in the same rice pot, layer rice with the mushroom mixture, starting and ending with rice (i.e. rice–mushroom–rice–mushroom–rice–mushroom–rice). Cover the pot and resume simmering on low heat for additional 10 minutes.

4   Serve with yogurt and *Shirazi* salad (p. 59).

Filo Pastry *Pulau/Polow*

Filo pastry rice cake

Serves 8

This dish is designed to impress. Flavorful rice encased in a flaky, melt-in-your-mouth pastry shell. Make this one at your next dinner party—it's sure to wow.

INGREDIENTS

1/2 cup	vermicelli
1/3 cup	olive oil
1 cup	protein of choice (seitan pictured)
2 cups	basmati rice, washed and drained
1/2 tsp	cinnamon, ground
pinch	cardamom, ground
4 cups	water
1 cup	peas
1 cup	carrots, cut into chunks
3	potatoes, cut into chunks
1/2	pack filo pastry
1 cup	slivered almonds or other nuts/ seeds
1 cup	raisins

DIRECTIONS

1   Preheat oven to 400F/200C.

2   Heat the oil in a pot on medium-high. Add the vermicelli and cook, stirring occasionally, until they reach a caramel-brown color. Strain the fried noodles, reserving the used oil.

3   Fry chosen protein in the reserved oil on medium heat until cooked through and slightly crispy on each side.

4   Add the rice, vermicelli, cinnamon, and cardamom. Sauté for two minutes.

5   Add the water to the saucepan. Carefully cover the pot with a dishtowel, which will help prevent steam from escaping. Then, fit the lid on the pot over the towel. Be very careful that no ends of the towel hang down the sides in reach of the flame.

6   Reduce heat to low and simmer for 20 minutes, until the water is completely absorbed and the rice has cooked fully.

7   While this is cooking, sauté the peas, carrots, and potato chunks in 1–2 T of oil on medium heat. The potatoes should be slightly golden.

8   In another pot, fry the nuts and raisin in oil for 4 minutes. Set 2 T aside for garnish.

(cont'd on next page)

9   Fold the remainder of the potato and remaining nut mixes into the rice until distributed evenly.

10   Spray or brush the inside of an oven-proof pot or tall casserol dish with olive or another oil.

11   Fill the pastry shell with the rice, using the back of a spoon to even out the top.

12   Fold the over-hanging corners of the pastry back towards the center of the rice.

13   Bake until the pastry turns golden, around 22 minutes. The "roof" will become crunchy and golden-brown, and will also make the task of flipping the rice easier. Remove from oven and set aside to cool.

14   Run a knife gently around the sides of the dish to pry any stuck pastry from the pot. Then, cool the bottom and sides of the pan under cold water, paying attention not to wet the inside. This will loosen the shell and make it easier to remove.

15   Place a large platter on top of the pot and, grasping the handles on each side (perhaps with assistance), flip the pot quickly and carefully so that the filo shell stands, inverted, on the platter.

16   Garnish with the remaining nuts and raisins.

Mujadarra

Rice with lentils and caramelized onions

Serves 5

Mujadarra, or lentil-rice, is a favorite across greater Syria, which includes Syria-proper, Jordan, Lebanon, and Palestine. Together, the combination of rice and lentils form a complete protein (containing all nine of the essential amino acids). Lentils are low in methionine and high in lysine, while rice is low in lysine and high in methionine. Mujadarra is extra decadent with an abundant embellishment of caramelized onions.

INGREDIENTS

1 cup	dry brown lentils, rinsed
1 cup	dry long-grain white basmati rice
1/4 cup	olive oil
3 large	white onions, diced
pinch	Arabic spice mix (*baharat*)
	salt and pepper, to taste

TO TOP

1 large	white onion, sliced
	olive oil
	slivered almonds

DIRECTIONS

1. Boil water in a saucepan. Add lentils and cook until boiling.

2. Turn down, cover and leave to simmer for 10 minutes. Drain.

3. Heat the olive oil in a frying pan and sauté 3 onions on medium-high, stirring occasionally until they caramelize. You want the onions to turn a rich, golden brown color.

4. Pour the rice into a bowl and fill it with warm water. Wash the grains with your hands until the water becomes cloudy. This is to eliminate some of the sticky, starch around the rice. Pour the water out and repeat the process four times.

5. Mix the rice, lentils, onions with 2 1/2 cups of water. Add salt and pepper, to taste.

6. Cover and simmer for 20 minutes. It's very important to keep the lid on at this stage so that the rice continues to steam.

7. In the meantime, heat oil in a pan. When sizzling, add the slices of the remaining onion and cook until they are crispy and brown (but not burned). These will form a caramel-like topping to garnish the rice with.

8. When the 20 minutes are over, remove the rice from heat and keep uncovered. Pour onto a dish and top with all the remaining onions.

9. Sprinkle almonds over and serve.

pp. 290–291: Globe. Photo: Peggy Marco, Pixabay.

pp. 292–293: Iranian desert, Golestan. Photo: Raandree, Pixabay

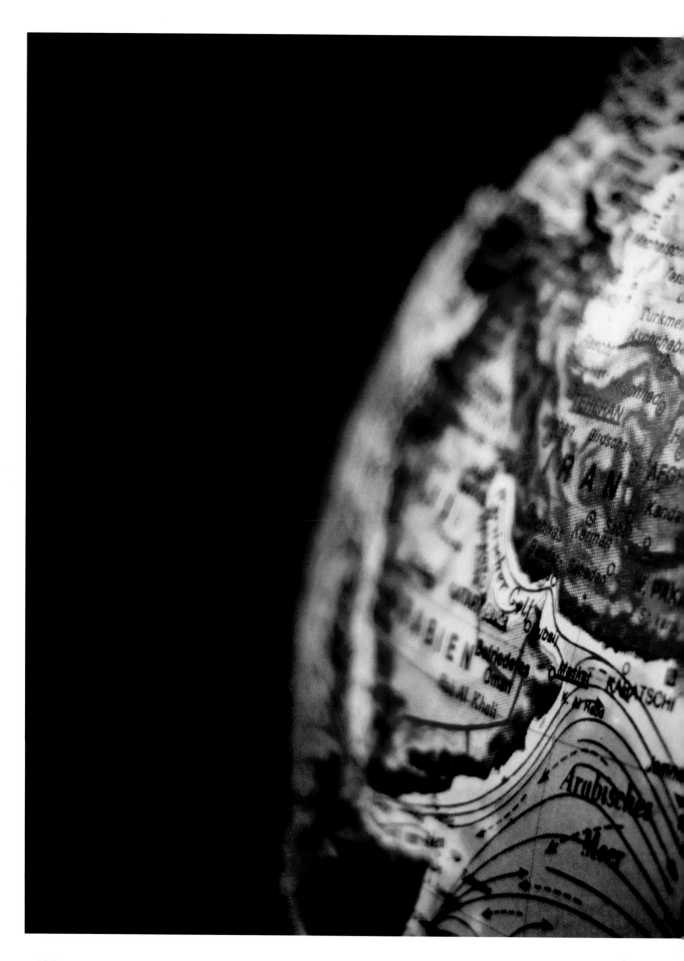

IRAN

The Land of the Magi; or, The Home of the Wise Men

Persian food is legendary throughout the Middle East and the world. The Royal Court kitchens are the antecedents of many of the world's cuisines, particularly those of the Middle East. There are many similarities, therefore, between Persian and certain Arabic foods. It must be said, however, that the historical term for "Persia" is fluid, and incorporates other regions outside of the contemporary Iranian state, such as Afghanistan and certain parts of the Indian subcontinent. South Asia possesses rich and varied culinary culture, which has evolved over centuries of movement and interaction, not least of all along the Caravansary (or *Karavansareh*).

The Persian *Khoresht* stew, which usually incorporates dried fruit and nuts, resembles the famed, aromatic Tagines of Morocco. The use of sweet or sour fruits with meat and vegetables, which results in a distinctly tart, fragrant flavor, can also be traced back to ancient Persian kitchens, which made their way to the Indian subcontinent in the Middle Ages, and even to other places such as Russia. Recipes for sweets such as *Kulfi*, or *polow* (rice dishes) flavored with stewed fruit, pistachios, walnuts, barberries, and saffron, were brought to India via the Mughal empire. It is for this reason that one can find dishes with the same names all across the world. *Burfi*, for instance, is derived from the Persian word for "snow," which it resembles. Chelo, Halva, Biryani, and Haleem are all examples of Persian foods that were incorporated into Indian cuisine, and which were innovated upon and localized. The exchange went both ways. The term *Basmati*, which is the most popular variety of rice in Iran, derives from the Sanskrit word for "fragrant," and was introduced to Persia by Indian merchants. The Russian *Piroshki* is known in Iran as *Pirashki*. Only, in a classically Persian move, the meat filling was replaced by a custard one.

Goldfish

It is a tradition in the festival of Nowruz (see next page) to place a goldfish in a bowl on the table, as a symbol of life renewing itself. In recent years, many Iranians, including the former president, have criticized the tradition, for which it is estimated that up to five million goldfish die. I, for one, hope that this tradition ends. You certainly don't have to have an animal on the table to celebrate the festival of Nowruz.

Persian Food as Medicine

The primacy of the anti-oxidant and nutrient-rich pomegranate also speaks to the medicinal quality of food in Iranian culture, as is the case in many other Eastern traditions. For example, the traditional concept of balancing "warm" and "cold" ingredients underlies the fundamental chemistry of Iranian dishes. "Warm" and "cold" signify how a food relates to the body's gut and metabolism. "Warm" foods are generally understood to be high-energy foods like dates, nuts, spices, and honey, while "cold" foods take more energy to digest, such as rice, yogurt, fruits, and vegetables. Therefore, when a child of Iranian descent complains of a stomach ache, most often the culprit will be a mix of two "cold" foods. Hence, most Iranian dishes were developed to consist of a healthy balance of the two categories. Rice is a common "cold" base in Iranian cuisine, so it is often embellished with "warm" spices, primarily saffron and turmeric. If the rice is not a dish by itself, it will usually be paired with a balanced stew made of nuts, vegetables, and meat.

Thirteen days after the Persian New Year, Nowruz, Iranians are culturally obligated to have an outdoor picnic, known as *Sizdah Bedar*, a tradition that unites all the essential elements of celebration according to Iranian standards: food, nature, and family. People gather outside with their loved ones, lay their sheets on grass sheltered by a blossoming tree, and decorate the ground with a rainbow of dishes already teasing stomachs with their wafted smells. In this moment, food is the centerpiece of togetherness. It is a universal magnet, attracting intimacy, laughter, pleasure, and positive energy.

—Hana Mahallati

Lubia Polow

Once balance is established within an Iranian dish, the external, esthetic aspect of the food is also addressed. Spices and herbs can thus serve two functions—creating balance, and beautifying the final product. For example, saffron is "warm" and is commonly used to decorate white rice. The dried barberries used in *zereshk polo* not only add flavor to rice, but also resemble little rubies embellishing a plain white canvas. The mint leaves in *mast-o-khiar* are often arranged to spell words or form a shape. Dried rose is also added to the yogurt-cucumber dip for an enhanced esthetic effect.

One of the most treasured dishes among Iranian children, *lubia polow*, or green bean rice, is arguably one of the most esthetically striking rice plates in Iranian cuisine. When made, it is the centerpiece of the table, a result of its vibrant colors: green, red, and gold. These are particularly festive colors, as green and red are in the Iranian flag. As follows, its external appeal reflects the well-balanced fusion of rice, spices, meat, and vegetables within. With *lubia polow* on the plate, the eyes, the nose, and the mouth are offered a blend of rich sensations that mirror the very flavors and colors that make up those moments we share around the picnic spread, under the trees, surrounded by those we love.

—**Hana Mahallati**
Iran, New York

p. 296: Islamic architecture. Photo: FatemehH, Pixabay

p. 297 (top): Blue tiles in Isfahan, Iran. Photo: Thieme, Pixabay

The pomegranate in particular, with its consistent reference in Iranian folklore, poetry, tiling, and jewelry, is colloquially understood as "the fruit of love" and is consequently the most popular fruit among Iranians.

—Hana Mahallati

Lubia Polow

Persian tomato and green-bean rice

Serves 5

"Lubia Polow is in Iran what ready-prepared mac and cheese is in the United States. This is what your mom or grandma would have ready when you came home from school: the ultimate comfort food. Everyone loves it, it's kid-friendly and yet totally delicious."

—**Roya**, The Farmacy Yoga & Pilates Studio, Marbella, Iran & USA

INGREDIENTS

2 cups	white basmati rice, rinsed
6 cups	water
1	large, white onion, chopped
3	cloves of garlic, ground
1 1/2 tsp	turmeric powder
1 tsp	advieh (Persian mixed spice)
1 tsp	paprika
1/2 tsp	cumin powder
1/2 tsp	ground pepper
1 tsp	thyme
1 tsp	salt
1 tsp	dried lime powder
1 cube	veggie stock, crushed
1/2 cup	tomato purée
2 1/2 T	olive oil + 1/4 cup
1 lb	green string beans ("lubia")
6 oz	tomato paste = 2 T
1/2 tsp	saffron, dissolved in 2 T hot water

DIRECTIONS

1. Bring water to a boil in a large pot with a pinch of salt and 1 T olive oil.

2. Add rice to boiling water and cook for 6 minutes. Stir and drain in cold water.

3. Heat 1 1/2 T olive oil in a large pot on medium-high. Add the onions and sauté until semi-translucent.

4. Add the garlic, spices, dried lime, and veggie stock and cook a further few minutes, stirring until the onions turn golden-brown.

5. Chop the green beans into pieces about one-inch long. Add them to the onions along with the tomato paste and tomato purée. Mix until combined. You may add 1/8–1/4 cup water if it seems dry.

6. Simmer for 12–15 minutes, until the beans reach a consistency that is more tender, but still retain some crunch. This is because the beans will continue to cook while the rice is steaming, so it is important that they not be overdone prior to the steaming process.

7. Pour 1/4 cup oil into a large pot. Spread several large spoonfuls of the rice across the bottom of pot. Add some of the bean mix, and then continue alternating layers until all the ingredients are used up.

8. Drizzle the saffron water all over the rice.

9. Sauté on high for 12 minutes, so that the bottom becomes crispy. This is known as "tahdig" in Farsi. Reduce the heat to low and simmer for 20 minutes. Do not lift the lid during this time

10. Serve with *Shirazi* salad (p. 59) and yogurt (pp. 67) and pickled vegetables.

Above: Desert at night. Photo: Henrivh, Pixabay

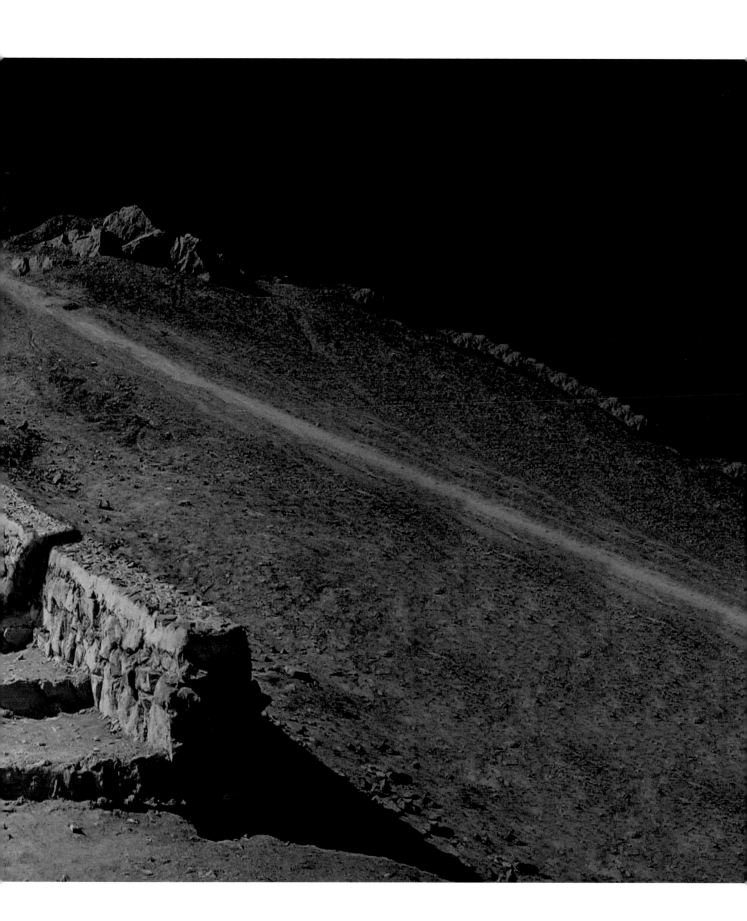

Dolmeh Felfel

Peppers stuffed with rice

Serves 5

Stuffed vegetables of every kind are found across the Middle East (see Stuffed Zucchini, p. 109) and the Mediterranean. They do not belong to any single place—but wherever this recipe is found, one will notice regional particularities that came about through the innovation and adaptation of the locals who incorporated these recipes into their culinary repertoires. Dolmeh is a generic Farsi word to describe stuffed vegetables or vine leaves. This recipe was taught to me by Soheila, a strong Iranian woman (and a phenomenal cook) whom I have had the pleasure of learning from and looking up to since I was a child.

INGREDIENTS

1/2 cup	lentils, dry
1 cup	basmati rice, dry
2	cloves of garlic, minced
1/4 cup	olive oil
1 cup	dried porcini mushrooms, soaked in warm water for 1 hour
1	large white onion, diced
1 T	paprika
1 T	turmeric
1/2 T	cinnamon
2 T	tomato paste = 6 oz
1/4 cup	wine or grape juice
6	bell peppers
2 cups	parsley, chopped
	dill, for garnish

SAUCE

400g	tomato paste = 1 3/4 cup
1 cup	water or stock
1 T	paprika
1/2 T	date syrup or sugar

DIRECTIONS

1   Boil lentils according to instructions, then drain and set aside.

2   Rinse the rice in warm water with your hands until the water runs clear.

3   Bring a saucepan to boil with four cups of water. Add the rice and cook on medium heat for 12 minutes. Remove from heat and drain.

4   Heat olive oil in a large saucepan with paprika, turmeric, and cinnamon. Drain the mushrooms and add them to the pan along with the tomato paste, parsley, garlic, onion, and wine. Stir occasionally to prevent burning.

5   When the onions are tender (approximately five minutes), add the semi-cooked rice to the mushroom mix. Cook on medium-low heat for eight minutes.

6   Wash your peppers and carefully cut a round hole around the stalk, as pictured. Remove the seeds from the middle and set the tops aside. Fill the peppers with the rice mixture and replace the caps.

7   Mix all the sauce ingredients and pour half of it into a large saucepan. Place the peppers upright inside the pot and pour the remaining sauce over them. Simmer, covered, on low for one hour.

8   When the dish is ready, arrange them with the sauce and garnish with chopped dill.

Home

no one leaves home unless

home is the mouth of a shark

you only run for the border

when you see the whole city running as well

your neighbors running faster than you

breath bloody in their throats

the boy you went to school with

who kissed you dizzy behind the old tin factory

is holding a gun bigger than his body

you only leave home

when home won't let you stay.

no one would leave home unless home chases you,

fire under feet,

hot blood in your belly.

it's not something you ever thought of doing,

until the blade burned threats into

your neck

and even then you carried the anthem under

your breath

only tearing up your passport in an airport toilet

sobbing as each mouthful of paper

made it clear that you would not be going back.

you have to understand,

no one puts their children in a boat

unless the water is safer than the land

no one burns their palms

under trains

beneath carriages

no one spends days and nights in the stomach of a truck

feeding on newspaper unless the miles traveled

means something more than journey.

no one crawls under fences

wants to be beaten

pitied

no one chooses refugee camps

or strip searches where your

body is left aching

or prison,

because prison is safer

than a city of fire

and one prison guard

in the night

is better than a truckload

of men who look like your father

no one could take it

no one could stomach it

no one's skin would be tough enough

the

go home blacks

refugees

dirty immigrants

asylum seekers

sucking our country dry

niggers with their hands out

they smell strange

savage

messed up their country and now they want

to mess ours up

how do the words

the dirty looks

roll off your backs

maybe because the blow is softer

than a limb torn off

or the words are more tender

than fourteen men between

your legs

or the insults are easier

to swallow

than rubble

than bone

than your child's body in pieces.

i want to go home,

but home is the mouth of a shark

home is the barrel of the gun

and no one would leave home

unless home chased you to the shore

unless home told you

to quicken your legs

leave your clothes behind

crawl through the desert

wade through the oceans

drown

save

be hungry

beg

no one leaves home until home is a sweaty voice
in your ear

saying—

leave,

run away from me now

i don't know what i've become

but i know that anywhere

is safer than here.

—Warsan Shire

Sweets

Baklava

Baklava is one of the most popular sweets in the Middle East, and is served at almost every occasion all over the region. It is thought to have originated with the Assyrians of Mesopotamia sometime around the eighth century BCE. There are many variations of baklava, though the ingredients are generally similar. Feel free to play around with different nuts. This flaky, nutty version is sugar-free, using honey or date syrup instead of sugar.

INGREDIENTS

1 packet	filo pastry, thawed
1 1/2 cups	walnuts
1/2 cup	pistachios
1 T	rosewater or orange blossom water
1/2 cup	margarine (unsalted) = 113.4 g or 8 T
2 T	date syrup or honey
optional	pinch nutmeg, cardamom, ground or cloves, ground

SYRUP

1 1/2 cups	date syrup or honey
3/4 cup	water
	skin of 1/2 lemon
1 T	rosewater
optional	pinch nutmeg, cardamom, ground or cloves, ground

DIRECTIONS

1. Preheat oven to 350F/180C.

2. Pulse the pistachios and the walnuts in a blender until ground into little pieces. Then mix with rosewater, the sweetener, and the spices.

3. Place one sheet of filo dough in a large dish. Brush with a layer of melted butter. Repeat this process with four more sheets of dough, brushing each with a layer of margarine.

4. Spread the nut mixture over the pan. Add five more layers of buttered dough on top. Bake for 30 minutes, until golden-brown.

5. Heat all the ingredients for the syrup in a saucepan over medium heat, stirring occasionally. When boiling, lower the heat and simmer for 10–15 minutes. Remove lemon skin.

6. With a sharp knife, cut the baklava into rectangular, triangular, or diamond-shaped pieces. Pour the syrup mix over the baklava as soon as it has been removed from the oven. Garnish with pistachio.

7. Can be stored in an airtight container for up to 2–3 weeks.

Qatayef

The origins of this sweet are contested, with some tracing them back to the Abbasid period (566–653 CE) and others claiming that they were first served during the Umayyad Era, in the eighth century. The word *qatayef* (or *'atayef* in some dialects) literally means "picked bites"—similar to the English "finger food."

Today, you can see *qatayef* being sold during the month of Ramadan on streets across the Arab world, from Cairo to Gaza. They are inexpensive to make, delicious and easy. *Qatayef* are usually filled with a coconut-walnut-cinnamon mix, a honey-nut mix, or cheese.

Qatayef Thuraya / قطايف ثريا

Pancakes stuffed with naturally sweetened date caramel

....

Sweet dumpling stuffed with sugar-free plant-based caramel. This recipe uses typical Middle Eastern flavors in a novel way, without any animal products—making it a perfect, vegan sweet. The date paste and tahini form a creamy caramel that is both decadent and packed with nutrients.

....

INGREDIENTS—DOUGH

1 1/2 cups	all-purpose flour
1 tsp	baking powder
1 T	sugar, agave, or date syrup
1 1/2 cups	warm water
pinch	salt

INGREDIENTS—ROSE SYRUP

	date syrup
	rosewater
	water

CARAMEL FILLING

1 cup	date paste, warmed to soften
1/2 cup	tahini
1/3 cup	coconut oil (optional)

Mix all ingredients and blend until smooth.

DIRECTIONS FOR PANCAKE

1   In a bowl, add all the dough ingredients except for the water. Using a whisk, mix until incorporated.

2   Gradually add the water, whisking all the while. Do this slowly in order to avoid lumps forming in the dough. The consistency should be a little bit thinner than pancake batter.

3   Set the mixture aside and allow it to rest for 30 minutes.

4   Once your dough has rested for 30 minutes, heat up a cast iron pan (or a non-stick pan), oil it slightly, and make small pancakes of around 10cm in diameter. Cook on one side until bubbles form but do not flip—the edges must be soft enough to stick together when pressed.

5   Transfer your pancakes to a tray and leave them to cool at room temperature.

ASSEMBLY

1   Place a spoonful of caramel in the center of each pancake.

2   Fold the sides into half moons, pressing along the edges to seal the dumpling.

3   Heat your pan to high and add 1 T neutral-tasting oil.

4   When the pan is sizzling hot, fry the 'atayef until golden-brown and crispy on both sides.

5   Transfer the cooked dumplings to a paper towel–lined plate to cool slightly. Serve drizzled with syrup and chopped nuts.

Wholegrain *Qatayef* with Macadamia and Coconut Cream

Wholegrain pancakes with dairy-free cream filling

This version of Qatayef uses a wholegrain dough, and is filled with a macadamia-coconut cream. The recipe is from Evergreen Organics, the first 100-percent vegan cafe in Doha, Qatar. Evergreen was founded on the belief that food is medicine. The chefs use the wonderfully rich flavors of traditional Middle Eastern cuisine to create beautiful plant-based dishes, such as Arabian Dream Chia Pudding, Chickpea Shakshouka, and Pomegranate-Pumpkin Salad with Dukkah and Date dressing. They, like Karavan, aim to create community centerd around shared knowledge, wellbeing, compassion, education, and inspiration. A true Karavansary!

INGREDIENTS—DOUGH

5/8 cup	oat flour*
1 cup	wholegrain flour
1/4 cup	cane sugar
1 tsp	baking powder
1 1/2 cups	water

MACADAMIA AND COCONUT FILLING

3/4 cup	macadamia (soaked for 8 hours)
1/3 cup	cashews (soaked for 8 hours)
1/3 cup	agave
30g	water
1/8 cup	orange blossom water
1/8 tsp	salt
1/3 cup	coconut cream

* Make your own oat flour by simply pulsing whole oats in a high powered blender or food processor

DIRECTIONS

1. Blend the nuts, agave, water, orange blossom, and salt in a high-powered blender. When the mixture is very smooth, transfer it to a dry bowl.

2. Whisk in the coconut cream. Cover and refrigerate for 2–3 hours, allowing it to set.

3. In a bowl, add all the dough ingredients except for the water. Use a whisk to mix until incorporated.

4. Gradually add the water, whisking all the while. Do this slowly in order to avoid lumps forming in the dough. The consistency should be a little bit thinner than pancake batter.

5. Set the mixture aside and allow it to rest for 30 minutes. Meanwhile, start your Macadamia and Coconut Filling.

6. Once your dough has rested for 30 minutes, heat up a cast-iron pan (or non-stick pan). Oil it slightly and make small pancakes of around 10cm in diameter. Cook on one side until bubbles form but do not flip—the edges must be soft and doughy enough to stick together when pressed.

7. Transfer the pancakes to a tray and leave them to cool at room temperature.

ASSEMBLAGE

1. Spoon around 45g of the Macadamia and Coconut Filling in the center of each pancake.

2. Close the qatayef from one end, forming a shape similar to an ice cream cone. Use toothpicks to hold it together.

3. Sprinkle chopped pistachio onto the open end and serve with a side of agave.

Mamounieh

Rose-flavored semolina pudding

INGREDIENTS

1 cup	coarse semolina
4 cups	water
1 1/2 cups	sugar
3 T	neutral oil (e.g., canola)
1 tsp	rosewater or orange blossom water

TO TOP

1/2 cup	chopped pistachios
	berries
	cinnamon
	other chopped, dried fruit

Mamounieh is a luscious breakfast and dessert pudding made from toasted semolina, nuts, and rosewater, and comes from the ancient city of Aleppo, in Syria. It is sometimes served with cream or bread, but this version is garnished with chopped pistachio and fruit.

DIRECTIONS

1. Make a simple sugar syrup by boiling the water and sugar together in a saucepan. When the water reaches a rolling boil, turn it down to simmer.

2. Meanwhile, heat the oil in a large pan. Toast the semolina on medium-high until it reaches a golden hue. Stir it with a wooden spoon to prevent burning.

3. Add the semolina to the water. Use the wooden spoon to stir until the mixture thickens—about three minutes. Turn off the heat and cover the saucepan for ten minutes.

4. Spoon the *mamounieh* into bowls and serve with nuts, fruit, and a sprinkle of cinnamon.

Kleicha

Iraqi date-and-nut-rolled cookies

Kleicha are considered the national cookie of Iraq. They are served at almost all occasions, and are typically enjoyed with tea or coffee. One can shape them rolled-up, as pictured, or in balls or crescents. This is a matter of personal preference, though the nut filling won't hold particularly well in the rolled-up form.

INGREDIENTS

2 cups	flour
2 T	sugar
1/2 tsp	baking powder
1/2 tsp	cardamom, ground
1/2 cup	butter or dairy-free substitute
1/2 cup	cold water
pinch	salt

DATE FILLING

1/2 cup	date paste or pitted dates, chopped finely
2 T	butter or vegan alternative
1 tsp	rose water
2 T	water

NUT FILLING

1/2 cup	almonds or walnuts, finely ground
2 T	melted butter or dairy-free alternative
2 T	honey or sugar
1 tsp	rose water
Optional:	2 cardamom pods, crushed

DIRECTIONS

1 Preheat oven to 350F/180C.

2 In a bowl, combine all the dry ingredients. Use your hands to rub in the butter until it is completely incorporated. You may use a food processor if you wish to expedite the process.

3 Add the water very gradually and roll the dough into a ball.

4 Knead until smooth and cover with a cloth. Leave the mixture for 40–60 minutes in a warm place. Meanwhile, get started on the date filling.

5 Dip your hands in a bowl of flower so that the mixture will not stick to them. Create golfball-sized balls of dough and use your thumb to imprint large pockets to hold the fillings.

6 Fill with either of the two filling options (date or nut) and then close the cavity. Traditionally, the cookie will be kept as a sphere if filled with dates or shaped into a crescent if filled with nuts.

7 Alternatively, you can roll out the dough into a rectangle (not too thick) on a lightly floured surface. Spread the date filling evenly over the dough using a wet spoon. Roll up the dough to form a long cylinder and slice it horizontally into pieces.

8 Bake for 20–30 minutes until golden around the edges. The exact cooking time is dependent on the shape and size of the cookies, so the best option is to turn on the oven light (if you have one), and check at 20, 25, and 30 minutes to make sure the cookies don't burn

Halawat Sha'riyya / حلاوة شعرية

Sweet, golden vermicelli noodles

Sha'riyya (also called *sha'eeriyya* in some Arab countries) is wheat noodles, similar to angel hair pasta. It is mostly sold in form of balls (also called "nests"), available at Middle Eastern stores (sometimes labeled "thin noodles #1"). For savory dishes, we break it and drop it into soup pots as a thickening agent, or fry it and let it steam with rice, as garnish. And in this enticing dessert of *halawat sha'riyya*, where it is the main ingredient, we keep the strands relatively long.

—**Nawal Nasrallah**, *Delights from the Garden of Eden*; NawalCooking.blogspot.com

....

According to Professor Nasrallah, the earliest-found reference to the term sha'riyyal *was in the fifteenth-century Syrian cookbook,* Kitab al-Tibakha, *written by the scholar Ibn al-Mubarrid. However, the pasta he refers to was probably more granular than the thin, angel-hair shape of contemporary* sha'riyya. *Nevertheless, the practice of making such pastas is long-established in the Middle East, with recipes for* itriya *pasta dating back to the thirteenth century. The Persian word for noodle,* reshteh, *referred to the fact that these noodles,* itriya, *looked like "fine strings."*

....

INGREDIENTS

1 1/2 T	butter or non-dairy equivalent
1 T	canola oil
4 oz or 6 "nests"	vermicelli
2 cups	hot water
3/4 cup	sugar
3/4 tsp	cardamom, ground
2 tsp	rosewater
1/3 cup	walnut pieces
1 T	pistachios, coarsely ground (for garnish)

DIRECTIONS

1   In a heavy pot over medium heat, melt the butter with the oil.

2   Lightly crush the vermicelli nests between your fingers. Add pieces to the pot, and cook them, stirring constantly, until golden-brown (about 5 minutes). Carefully pour in the hot water, add the salt, and stir.

3   Bring the mixture to a boil, then lower the heat and simmer, covered, until the noodles start to soften (4–5 minutes).

4   Add the sugar, cardamom, rosewater, and walnuts. Stir until the sugar crystals dissolve. Then, let the mixture simmer, covered, on medium-low, gently stirring 2 or 3 times until moisture is absorbed, noodles look glossy, and the sugar starts to caramelize and stick to the bottom of the pot (12–15 minutes).

5   Invert the pot over a flat platter and spread the noodles, evening the surface with the back of a spoon. Sprinkle with ground pistachios, divide into portions, and serve warm. Leftovers may be refrigerated and then heated for 1 minute in the microwave.

Food Photography

Bibliography

Abdikarim, Shukri and Abderazzaq Noor. "The Somali Kitchen." www.somalikitchen.com.

Amnesty International. "50 Years of Israeli Occupation: Four Outrageous Facts about Military Order 101," by Nadine Marroushi, August 25, 2017, https://www.amnesty.org/en/latest/campaigns/2017/08/50-years-of-israeli-occupation-four-outrageous-facts-about-military-order-101.

Bennet, James. "No Terror This Time, Just Five Arab Cousins Taking a Deadly Gamble for Work," *New York Times*, December 14, 2002.

Bottéro, Jean. *The Oldest Cuisine in the World: Cooking in Mesopotamia.* Translate by Teresa Lavender Fagan. (Chicago: University of Chicago Press, 2004).

Coats, C. David. *Old MacDonald's Factory Farm: The Myth of the Traditional Farm and the Shocking Truth about Today's Agribusiness*. (New York: Continuum, 1989).

Francione, Gary and Anna Charlton. *The Abolitionist Approach to Animal Rights*. (Newark, NJ: Exempla Press, 2015).

Garfield, Richard. *The Impact of Economic Sanctions on Health and Well-Being*. Network Paper 31 of the Relief and Rehabilitation Network (RRN): 1-34. (London: Overseas Development Institute, 1999).

Hanafi, Sari. Spacio-cide: Colonial Politics, Invisibility and Rezoning in Palestinian Territory. *Contemporary Arab Affairs* 2(1): pp. 106–121.

Nasrallah, Nawal. *Delights from the Garden of Eden: A Cookbook and History of the Iraqi Cuisine.* Second edition. (Sheffield, UK: Equinox Publishing, 2013).

—— . "Iraqi Cuisine." In Christensen, Karen (ed). *Asian Cuisines: Food Culture from East Asia to Turkey and Afghanistan* (Great Barrington, MA: Berkshire Publishing Group, 2019), pp. 102–106.

Niblock, Tim. *Pariah States & Sanctions in the Middle East: Iraq, Libya, Sudan (The Middle East in the International System.* (Boulder, CO: Lynne Rienner Publishers, 2001).

Olmsted, Jennifer. "Globalization Denied: Gender and Poverty in Iraq and Palestine." In Reese, Ellen, Waller, Marguerite, Cabezas Amalia I. *Wages of Empire: Neoliberal Policies, Repression, and Women's Poverty*. (United Kingdom: Taylor & Francis, 2015), pp. 178–189.

Steiner, Gary. *Animals and the Moral Community: Mental Life, Moral Status, and Kinship*. (New York: Columbia University Press, 2008).

Twitty, Michael. *The Cooking Gene*. (New York: Harper Collins, 2017).

UNSCO (UN Special Coordinator for the Middle East Peace Process). "UN: New Economic Figures for West Bank and Gaza Show Rapid Deterioration Leading to Human Catastrophe," Press Release, August 29, 2002, https://reliefweb.int/report/israel/un-new-economic-figures-west-bank-and-gaza-show-rapid-deterioration-leading-human.

Wollen, Phillip. "Animals Should Be Off the Menu." Speech given to the St. James Ethics Centre and Wheeler Centre Debate. Sydney, Autralia. May 16, 2012.

World Bank 2003. *Twenty-Seven Months: Intifada, Closures, and Palestinian Economic Crisis—An Assessment*, https://documents1.worldbank.org/curated/en/616581468765333893/pdf/263141270months0Intifada10Closures.pdf.

World Bank 2004. *Deep Palestinian Poverty in the Midst of Economic Crisis*. Co-published with the Palestinian Central Bureau of Statistics, https://documents1.worldbank.org/curated/en/935421468780339774/pdf/307510Eng.pdf.

Visualizing Impact. "Visualizing Palestine." https://www.visualizingpalestine.org.

Index

Acknowledgments

The Karavan Kitchen cookbook was assembled over the course of two years, with the help of many individuals, for whom Soraya and the whole Karavan team are incredibly grateful. The author would like to acknowledge the incredible work of the team at Lantern Publishing & Media, especially Martin Rowe, Emily Lavieri-Scull, Pauline Lafosse, and Liza Barkova. The proceeds from this book go towards Karavan's mission to use technology to empower humanity's most vulnerable.

If you enjoyed these recipes, we would highly appreciate if you would be so kind as to share your experiences/thoughts/images on social media and encourage others to contribute to our cause. Every dollar counts, and we are on a mission to create a platform that contributes to a more just, more fair world than the one that witnesses these unprecedented levels of displacement.

If you would like to know more about what we are doing, visit our website at www.karavanfoundation.org, where you can sign up for our mailing list.

Many thanks again for supporting our project. We will always be grateful to those who invested in us in these early stages. You are the reason we have a chance to try and build an innovative solution that addresses the needs of displaced people in the most dignified, empowering, and advantageous way.

Permissions

Mahmoud Darwish's poem "In Jerusalem" from *The Butterfly's Burden* is translated by Fady Joudah. Copyright © 2008 by Mahmoud Darwish. Translation copyright © 2007 by Fady Joudah. Reprinted with the permission of The Permissions Company, LLC on behalf of Copper Canyon Press, www.coppercanyonpress.org.

The poem "Everything" by Al-Saddiq Al-Raddi is used with permission from *Poems*, published by Enitharmon Press in 2008. The translation is by Sarah Maguire and Sabry Hafez.

The poem "Home" by Warsan Shire is widely available on the Internet, and you can see her reading the poem on YouTube: https://www.youtube.com/watch?v=nl9D92Xiygo. Warsan Shire can be followed on Twitter at warsan_shire. Her website is: http://warsanshire.squarespace.com.

About the Publisher

Lantern Publishing & Media was founded in 2020 to follow and expand on the legacy of Lantern Books—a publishing company started in 1999 on the principles of living with a greater depth and commitment to the preservation of the natural world. Like its predecessor, Lantern Publishing & Media produces books on animal advocacy, veganism, religion, social justice, humane education, psychology, family therapy, and recovery. Lantern is dedicated to printing in the United States on recycled paper and saving resources in our day-to-day operations. Our titles are also available as ebooks and audiobooks.

To catch up on Lantern's publishing program, visit us at www.lanternpm.org.

facebook.com/lanternpm
instagram.com/lanternpm
twitter.com/lanternpm